UNITED IN RIVALRY

UNITED IN RIVALRY

RICHMOND'S ARMSTRONG-MAGGIE WALKER CLASSIC

MICHAEL WHITT

THE History PRESS

Published by The History Press
Charleston, SC 29403
www.historypress.net

First published 2009

Manufactured in the United States

ISBN 978.1.59629.654.1

Library of Congress CIP data applied for.

Notice: The information in this book is true and complete to the best of our knowledge. It is offered without guarantee on the part of the author or The History Press. The author and The History Press disclaim all liability in connection with the use of this book.

Ladies and gentlemen, welcome to this year's Armstrong-Walker Classic.
Will you please rise for the playing of our National Anthem?
—France M. Brinkley, Official Game Announcer

Contents

Preface

To understand high school football, you need to see it, as longtime coach John Trott once told me, as "a game played by teenage boys where the ball's not round." That said, it is also a game that brings towns, counties and neighborhoods together. And for forty-one years in Richmond, Virginia, one game united a community off the field in such a way that it could never divide it on the field.

Starting as an afterthought at the end of the 1938 season, on Friday, December 2 Armstrong High School faced Maggie L. Walker High School on the gridiron for a football game. What began as a bunch of inexperienced underclassmen at newly opened Walker challenging well-established Armstrong in a football contest turned into one of the greatest traditions in a city that loved its traditions.

But this tradition was different in a city that prided itself on having been the capital of the Confederacy and which contained the "largest collection of second-place trophies" in the nation, known as Monument Avenue.

Armstrong and Maggie Walker High Schools were the African American stepchildren of the Richmond school system. In an age when the last vestiges of Jim Crow and "Colored Only" signs still dictated where people could go and when, the two schools were the only places the grandchildren—and later, great-grandchildren—of the slaves and freedmen who had worked in the homes, carriage houses and fields of Richmond's white population could go for an education.

What they gave to the community with that last game of the season was a rich tradition of festivities and activities and a football game that became as much a part of Richmond's history as the Civil War. They gave Richmond the "Classic."

Acknowledgements

Special thanks go to Wendy Addison; Sonya Anani; Fred Anderson; Coach Lou Anderson; Randy Ashe; the Boatwright Library at the University of Richmond; Eva Brinkley, for the use of her Armstrong yearbooks; Temple Cabell; Bennie Callaham; P.J. Callaham, for the use of his Maggie L. Walker yearbooks; CC2; John Dorman; Melissa Foster; Barksdale Haggins; Melvin Jones; the Library of Virginia; Charles Mike; Bill Millsaps; Tom Mitchell; Mom; Vicki Olsen; Dale Parrish; Chester Porter; the Richmond Public Library; Coach Ulis Shelton; Les Smith; Dr. Jerry Tarver; Ray "Float" Taylor; Dr. Welford Taylor; Coach John Trott; Art Utley; the Virginia Historical Society; Vlad; Richard Waller Jr.; John Whiting of Whiting's Old Paper; the late Reverend Robert A. Whitt; John Williams Jr.; Lavern Brown Williams; and Patti Yaman.

Pregame

Late 1863

Lieutenant Colonel Samuel C. Armstrong, born in 1839 to missionary parents in Hawaii, was assigned to the Ninth Regiment, United States Colored Troops.

September 1865

In the shadows of a burned-out Richmond, just five months after the fall of the Confederate States of America, the Freedman's Bureau founded the first free schools for the recently freed African American children of Richmond. At first, the teaching was done at four churches and Dill's Bakery, located at the corner of St. James and Clay Streets.

White female teachers from the North joined the superintendent of the schools, Union army chaplain Rabza Morse Manley, as children were taught during the day and adults at night.

July 17, 1867

Maggie Lena Walker was born to Elizabeth Draper, a former assistant cook in the Church Hill home of Elizabeth Van Lew, a Unionist who ran a spy ring in the shadow of the Confederate capitol building. Walker's father was Eccles Cuthbert, an Irish-born newspaperman and abolitionist.

September 17, 1867

The Richmond Colored High School and Normal School, located at the corner of Sixth and Duval Streets, was dedicated. Manley was named the principal, and the teachers remained northern white women.

Brevet Brigadier-General Samuel C. Armstrong. *1957* Armstrong Rabza.

The Maggie L. Walker House. *Photo by Michael Whitt.*

Maggie L. Walker. *1975* Maggie L. Walker Dragon.

1868

Hampton Normal and Agricultural Institute was founded by Armstrong, who, since 1866, had been supervising the establishment of freedmen schools in eastern Virginia.

APRIL 1873

Having outgrown the building at Sixth and Duval, the Richmond Colored High School and Normal School relocated to a newly erected building at the end of Twelfth Street and opened with a student body of 113 pupils.

SPRING 1883

Maggie Walker graduated with honors from Richmond Colored High and Normal School and began teaching at the Lancaster Elementary School. She also began studying accounting at night school.

MAY 11, 1893

Samuel Armstrong died and was buried at the Hampton Institute campus cemetery.

NOVEMBER 2, 1903

Maggie Walker opened the St. Luke Penny Savings Bank, the first bank owned and operated by African Americans.

1909

After the Twelfth Street building was condemned in 1908, and after a year housed in the Baker Street School building, the Richmond Colored High School and Normal School moved to the corner of First and Leigh Streets and was renamed Armstrong High School in honor of Samuel Armstrong.

SEPTEMBER 8, 1915

After being accredited as a four-year high school in 1912, the white faculty at Armstrong High School was replaced with fifteen African American teachers.

First and Leigh Streets, site of the first Armstrong High School, 1908–22. *Photo by Michael Whitt.*

Prentis and Leigh Streets, site of Armstrong High School, 1922–52. *Photo by Michael Whitt.*

SEPTEMBER 1923

Due to an expanding student body, Armstrong High School was forced to relocate again and moved to Prentis and Leigh Streets.

1930

The St. Luke Penny Savings Bank merged with two other black-owned banks in Richmond to form the Consolidated Bank and Trust Company, with Maggie Walker named as chairperson.

SEPTEMBER 1933

After the football program had been dropped in 1929 because of economic difficulties brought on by the Great Depression, a group of Armstrong students petitioned the Richmond School Board to reestablish the program. A total of $187.50 was raised, a team was fielded and science teacher Maxie Robinson, an Armstrong graduate, was named as coach. That season, Armstrong finished with five wins and no losses.

Consolidated Bank today. *Photo by Michael Whitt.*

Cover of 1934 *Spirit of Armstong. Courtesy of John Dorman.*

Lombardy and Leigh Streets, site of Maggie L. Walker High School. *1975* Maggie L. Walker Dragon.

December 15, 1934

Maggie Lena Walker died and was buried at Richmond's Evergreen Cemetery.

1936

The Richmond City School Board voted to open a second African American high school providing a vocational and industrial education.

September 8, 1938

The doors of Maggie L. Walker High School were opened.

SECTION I

First Quarter

(1938–1949)

The First Meeting

December 2, 1938

The first Armstrong–Maggie Walker game wasn't even on the schedule in 1938. In fact, of the two soon-to-be rivals, only Armstrong had a schedule. Maggie Walker was in its initial year as a school, and while Coach Arthur "Stretch" Gardner was helping teach skills of the game to his young, inexperienced group, which was eager to learn, no games were planned. Practice was nothing more than preparation for the 1939 season.

But two weeks before Thanksgiving, Gardner, urged by his players, approached Armstrong coach Maxie Robinson about the possibility of a game between the schools. The Wildcat staff, including Harry Williams, worked out the details, and Friday, December 2, was chosen as the date. Hovey Field, on the campus of Virginia Union University, was the site.

On the afternoon of the game, the Walker squad walked down the street, and Armstrong's Wildcats, wearing their distinctive orange and blue uniforms, traveled from Prentis and Leigh, along with between two and five thousand spectators (depending on whom you asked), to the field.

Unfortunately, no one in the media was there to report the outcome.

When the teams met, Armstrong had enjoyed a successful 5-2-0 season, which included a win over rival Peabody of Petersburg. Walker on the other hand, had to borrow fifteen to twenty red and white (the official

THE SPIRIT OF ARMSTRONG Page Twenty-One

SPORTS

ARMSTRONG FOOTBALL SQUAD 1933-1934

SUMMARY OF ARMSTRONG'S SPORTS FROM SEPTEMBER, '33 TO JUNE '34

By Wilbert Foster

In September when school opened, Armstrong could not boast of having a football team. A group of boys met and decided they wanted to have a football team. They saw Mr. Binford about having the team. They were informed by Mr. Binford that if they raised a certain sum they would received an additional sum from the board. The Athletic Association was formed. The student body and friends raised nearly twice the sum designated by Mr. Binford, under the supervision of the Athletic Committee.

The boys could have the football team but who would coach the team? Then Maxie Robinson, former Armstrong High and Virginia Union star, volunteered his services as coach. When he issued a call for candidates, between forty and fifty candidates responded.

After preparing for their first game, the team journeyed to Blackstone for their first game. They swamped Nottaway 54-0. Armstrong then played their first home game. They defeated John Moncure 82-0.

The next game was with a tougher foe, when Nansemond bowed to Armstrong. The score of this game was 13-7. Armstrong defeated their toughest foe, Huntington High, of Newport News, for the first time. The score of this thriller was 12-6.

Armstrong met Moncure in a return game and easily defeated them the second time, 32-0.

Armstrong had a successful season, winning 5 and losing 0. Armstrong scored 193 points against 13 for opponents. On December 18, 1933 eighteen members of the football squad were awarded the varsity letter "A".

The boys then turned their minds to basketball. When Coach Williams issued the call for candidates, thirty cagers responded.

The team entered the Basketball Tournament held at Virginia State College, March 9-10. For the first time in history of the tournament, Armstrong advanced to the finals only to bow to Dunbar 40-20.

Armstrong advanced to the finals when they won from Nansemond Institute, by forfeit (2-0) when Nansemond failed to appear on the court. Armstrong met Addison and eked out a thrilling victory over the Roanoke cagers. After the game between Armstrong and Dunbar, the members of the former team

MR. MAXIE ROBINSON
Football Coach

An account of the 1933 Armstrong football season. *Courtesy of John Dorman.*

school colors were green and white) uniforms from a local recreation center to field its team.

Standouts on the 1938 Armstrong team were runners Marion Robinson and "Flash" Gordon. Joining these two in the backfield were quarterback Douggie Patterson, halfback Brightwell Ellis, fullback Clifton Price and Joe Turpin, who doubled as the Wildcats' kicker.

Most of Patterson's passes went to end Morris Taylor, while junior Robert Moore, a five-foot, seven-inch, 170-pounder who played guard, anchored the line. Other Wildcats of note were linemen Anthony James, Benny Duckenfield, Joe Washington, Elliott Athey and Purcell Taylor.

Although much younger, the Dragons boasted running back "Catfish" Battle, 235-pound lineman Warren Arvin and kicker/end William Mann. Joining Battle in the backfield were Dooley Harvey, Sam Cunningham and Daniel Cameron.

As for the game, few actual facts have survived; we don't even know the exact score. The official records report that Armstrong won 26–0, but some eyewitnesses recall a final tally of 25–0.

Robinson scored twice, as did Wilbert "Flash" Brown, for the Wildcat touchdowns, but who scored the extra points was never recorded.

The only thing that was certain was that a rivalry had been born.

"Segregation of Schools According to Race a Wise Policy"

December 2, 1939

After the success of what could almost be called a pickup game in 1938, the athletic committees of Armstrong and Maggie Walker approached the City of Richmond's school board with a request that the 1939 contest be played at the John Marshall (JM) High School stadium located near the old JM downtown campus. All that was asked for was the use of the field, not the lockers or showers.

J.H. Binford, who spoke for the board, said that the use of the white facility for the game was inappropriate since the board felt that "segregation of schools according to race [was] a wise policy." Thus, for a second year, the teams paid Virginia Union University a fee for the use of Hovey Field for the contest.

A crowd of thirty-five hundred gathered to watch the 4-1-1 Wildcats and the 1-1-2 Green Dragons face off on a mild yet overcast day that would soon turn to rain, muddying the field.

It was the Dragons who first threatened in the opening period when William Mann attempted a forty-yard field goal that was blocked by Walker's Ernest Anderson. Then the Wildcats' Douggie Patterson, moving the ball to the Walker twenty-five, tossed a pass to Joe Turpin, who caught the ball and fumbled. Picking the ball up, he headed left, changed to the right and ran into the end zone standing up. Anderson blocked the PAT (point after touchdown) kick, and the Wildcats entered the second period up 6–0.

In the second period, the Wildcats drove to the Walker ten, where Anderson ran for the score to put Armstrong up 12–0.

On the ensuing kickoff, quarterback James Moore returned the ball to his thirty-seven. But then David Cameron fumbled when hit by Leroy McAllister,

uesday, November 29, 1938 — *News of Colored People*

Plans Complete For Meeting Of Baptists

Final arrangements for the reat Baptist fellowship meeting, hich will open tomorrow morning at Sixth Mt. Zion Baptist hurch. for a two-day session, ere announced at the weekly ession of the Baptist Ministers' onference of Richmond and Vinity held at noon yesterday in benezer Baptist Church. The loal committee of arrangements is omposed of the Rev. W. L. Ranome, the Rev. W. T. Johnson and e Rev. C. C. Scott, president of e conference.

Prominent Baptists will be here om all parts of the State and rangements have been made to rve meals in the church for all sitors. The Rev. O. J. Allen, resident of the Baptist General ssociation, and the Rev. C. P. adison, president of the Virginia aptist State Convention, both of orfolk, will preside over the sesons.

The sessions will begin at 9:30 . M. daily and special meetings ill be held at 8 P. M. The public as been invited to join in the tivities.

Garden Club News

GET NEW ASSIGNMENTS—Rufus Lewis (left) and his assistant, Otis H. Bradley, who have been appointed by L. M. Kidd to have charge of the distribution and operation of music appliances in the colored sections. Mr. Lewis is the well known proprietor of the Barbecue Inn.

Armstrong, Walker Squads Prep for Tilt

Armstrong Wildcats held blackboard drills yesterday in preparation for their clash with the Walker High Dragons Friday afternoon at Hovey Field. Coach Maxie Robinson will hold hard drills today and tomorrow, drilling mainly players who will form the nucleus for next year's team.

Clifton Price, 145 pound fullback, Anthony James, 148 pound center, and Benny Duckenfield, 135 pound guard, are the only seniors scheduled to start. However, Wilbert (Flash) Brown, Marion Robertson, senior backs, and Joe Washington, Elliott Athey, and Purcell Taylor, senior lineman, will be in uniform.

The Dragons held extensive line drills yesterday as they went through drills designed to halt the vaunted Orange and Blue offensive, which led them to five victories this season. Considerable stress was put on the Wildcats famed "spread formation" which has played havoc with all opponents this season. Coaches Stretch Gardner and Harry (Cool) Williams semed set on the backfield combination of "Catfish" Battle, Dooley Harvey, Son Cunningham and Danny Cameron, which will match the A's combination in weight and speed, but not experience.

The first reference to the Armstrong–Maggie Walker game, *Richmond Times-Dispatch,* November 28, 1938. *Courtesy of Whiting's Old Paper.*

and the Wildcats recovered. Moving the ball to the five, Armstrong was denied a third first-half score when David Battle downed Wynder at the three, and the half ended with Armstrong up 12–0.

For most of the third quarter, the teams battled the elements as much as each other, with rain beginning to turn the field sloppy. The Wildcats reached the Dragon one on a pass from Patterson to Turpin. On the first play of the final period, Wynder ran the ball in, and Armstrong went up 18–0.

Turpin made Armstrong's final score on a fifty-five-yard double reverse before Walker averted a shutout when Julian Tyler pulled in a pass from Cameron, and the second Armstrong game ended with the Wildcats winning 24–6.

Armstrong	6	6	0	12	**24**
Maggie Walker	0	0	0	6	**6**

A: Turpin twenty-five-yard run (kick failed)
A: Anderson ten-yard run (PAT failed)
A: Wynder one-yard run (PAT failed)
A: Turpin fifty-five-yard run (PAT failed)
W: Tyler pass from Cameron (PAT failed)

Two Firsts and a Last

December 7, 1940

As in the 1938 contest, the 1940 meeting of Armstrong and Maggie Walker was almost completely overlooked by the media, and little exact information has survived. But the results did represent two key firsts. In the December 7 edition of the *Richmond Times-Dispatch*, a very brief article reported that "Walker High Beats Armstrong 13–6."

With three thousand spectators gathered at Hovey Field on December 6, the weather cooperated as the temperature hovered in the fifties and the skies remained clear.

Walker High Beats Armstrong, 13-6

The Maggie Walker High School football team defeated Armstrong High, 13-6, at Hovey Field yesterday before 3,000 spectators.

The lone score in the first half was made by Walker's Cameron, who dived over from the 4-yard line. The kick for extra point failed.

Armstrong scored its only touchdown in the third quarter, Morris Taylor receiving a pass over the goal for the tally. The try for extra point failed and the score remained tied at 6-6 until late in the fourth quarter when Arvin climaxed a long Walker march by plunging over from the 3-yard line. Arvin also accounted for the extra point with a line buck.

Lineups:

Pos.	Walker 13	Armstrong 6
L.E.	Anderson	Matthews
L.G.	D. Battle	Ruffin
L.T.	Joyner	Moore
C.	Yates	Bradley
R.G.	Boone	Moore
R.T.	Rogers	Green
R.E.	P. Johnson	Taylor
Q.B.	Cameron	Smith
H.B.	Mayo	Graham
H.B.	R. Johnson	Mann
F.B.	Arvin	Rainey

By periods:

Walker	0	6	0	7	—13
Armstrong	0	0	6	0	— 6

The first account of the Armstrong–Maggie Walker game in the *Richmond Times-Dispatch Sports Section*, December 8, 1940. *Courtesy of Boatwright Memorial Library, University of Richmond Archives.*

After a scoreless opening period, the Dragons got on the scoreboard first when Daniel Cameron bulled over on a four-yard run. The PAT kick failed, and Walker took a 6–0 advantage into intermission.

In the third quarter, the Wildcats pulled even when Morris Taylor grabbed a touchdown pass, and the teams appeared headed for a tie until the Dragons scored late in the final period,

Driving to the Armstrong three as the clock was running out, Warren Arvin scored and then ran in the conversion to give the Dragons their first ever series win, 13–6.

The contest also marked a last, as this third meeting was the final time the game would be played at Hovey.

Maggie Walker	0	6	0	7	**13**
Armstrong	0	0	6	0	**6**

W: Cameron four-yard run (kick failed)
A: Taylor catch (PAT failed)
W: Arvin three-yard run (Arvin run)

A New Home

November 22, 1941

After three years at Hovey Field, it was determined that the fourth Armstrong–Maggie Walker showdown needed a larger venue, and the game was moved to City Stadium, where it would stay for the duration.

As the day of the game approached, both teams' rosters were hit when the first peacetime military draft was called and the need to work took several players off the practice fields.

The first senior class in Walker's history had won three games to open the season before losing twice and tying once. Armstrong had suffered five straight losses, followed by back-to-back wins. For the first time, Walker entered the game favored to win as seven thousand spectators watched.

After a first half that was as bland as the overcast sky was gray, it was the underdog Wildcats who struck first in the third quarter.

Daniel Cameron got off a punt for Walker that was received by Nicholson. Nicholson headed one way and handed off to Reese going the other, and Reese broke free to advance the ball fifteen yards.

On the play, Cameron was hurt and was sidelined; nevertheless, the Wildcats advanced to the Dragon thirty-five. There, Crittenden, the Armstrong center, snapped the ball directly to George Smith, who faked one way, headed the other and didn't stop until he crossed the goal line for the game's first score.

David Battle blocked Smith's PAT kick, and as the teams changed possession, Armstrong was up 6–0.

Before the quarter was over, the Wildcats struck again when Nicholson, heading one way, handed off to Lawrence Hubbard on a reverse. Tucking the ball tightly, the fullback ran thirty-five yards into the end zone.

Raymond Starkes blocked Smith's extra point kick, and as the game entered the final period, Armstrong was up 12–0.

Maggie Walker put together a drive, or rather used three consecutive holding calls against Armstrong, to advance the ball forty-five yards, but the Wildcats' defense held, giving the offense one more shot.

Taking advantage of that shot, Linwood Scott tossed a pass to Nicholson, who quickly lateralled the ball to Hubbard. Hubbard broke free for the third Wildcat score.

The 1942 Maggie Walker coaching staff. *From left to right*: Allen Gaskins, Arthur "Stretch" Gardner and John "Pop" Williams. *1966* Maggie L. Walker Dragon.

From there, Armstrong ran out the clock. The team left the field an 18–0 winner and holder of three of the four championships and the O.P. Chiles Trophy, sponsored by Chiles Funeral Home.

Key to the win was Coach Robinson's use of the unfamiliar *T*-formation, the same formation that the Chicago Bears employed to defeat the Washington Redskins 73–0 in the National Football League Championship game in 1940.

None who left the stadium that afternoon cared that in just fifteen days, it would be December 7, 1941.

Armstrong	0	0	12	6	**18**
Maggie Walker	0	0	0	0	**0**

A: Smith thirty-five-yard run (Smith kick blocked)
A: Hubbard run (PAT failed)
A: Hubbard run off lateral from Nicholson (PAT failed)

Honoring Those Not There

November 21, 1942

With World War II raging overseas, the headlines of the Saturday, November 21 *Richmond Times-Dispatch* reported that the American navy won the Battle of the Solomon Islands and that German forces were pinned back for a decisive battle in Tunis. In Richmond, after five years, the Maggie Walker–Armstrong game was given the name "Classic."

In his article in the *Richmond Afro-American* the week after the game, R.H. Johnson stated:

> *The Green Dragons of Maggie L. Walker upset Coach Maxie Robinson's favored Armstrong High School Wildcats by a score of 7 to 6 in the thrill-packed fifth renewal of the city classic on Saturday…before a record-breaking crowd of approximately 8,000 spectators, about 1500 of whom were white.*

After the game went through an uneventful opening period, the attending crowd finally saw some action in the second quarter.

In possession near their own goal line, the Wildcats turned the ball over when Spencer, who had played for Walker in 1941, fumbled at his own seventeen and the Dragons recovered.

Henry Mayo ran two straight slants off tackle that moved the ball to the seven and gave the Dragons a first and goal.

J. Harris then gained two yards to the five. On the ensuing play, Harris got the ball and bulled over into the Wildcat end zone for the touchdown. He then tossed the extra point pass to Floyd Langhorne, and the Dragons were up 7–0. They held on to that advantage entering intermission.

The halftime show was dedicated to those alumni serving in the war effort. The bands played and the cadet corps marched.

In the third period, Maggie Walker was hit with a major penalty for illegal use of hands and was forced into a punting situation.

Harris took the snap, but the kick was blocked and William Causie-Estko recovered for the Wildcats at the Dragon twenty-five.

The 1942 Armstrong Wildcat football team. *1943* Armstrong Rabza.

After Leonard Scott advanced the ball five yards to the twenty, Joseph Banian was dropped for a three-yard loss back at the twenty-three.

On third and eight, Scott took the handoff, fumbled the ball, recovered it on the bounce and covered twenty yards to the three for a Wildcat first down.

Faced with a first and goal, Scott got the call and ran three yards off tackle into the end zone.

Down 7–6, the Wildcats went to the air for the tying extra point, but Harris's pass to Scott fell harmlessly to the turf, and the Dragons entered the final period up by one.

Armstrong wasn't done yet and drove to the Walker one before being turned back inches short of the goal by a tremendous stand by the Dragons.

A final Wildcat gasp for the win was stopped when Wilbert Truman intercepted a pass at his own forty-six and returned the ball to the Armstrong nine as the clock ran out. Walker had the upset win and its second Classic title.

Maggie Walker	0	7	0	0	**7**
Armstrong	0	0	6	0	**6**

W: Harris five-yard run (Langhorne pass from Harris)
A: Scott three-yard run (pass failed)

Two Teams, No Champion

November 20, 1943

The 1943 Classic opened on a warm, clear day with ten thousand spectators in the stands. The record crowd was drawn because, for the first time, both Armstrong and Maggie Walker entered the game undefeated. The Wildcats were 4-0-1 and the Dragons 6-0-1. When the afternoon was over, both remained undefeated.

In the first quarter, Walker had possession at its own forty. A long run by Wilbert Truman moved the ball deep into Wildcat territory. Several plays later, he bulled over from the three to give the Dragons a 6–0 advantage. Ray Blount's run for the extra point failed, and the quarter ended with Walker holding a one-touchdown lead.

The Wildcats owned the second period as the running of Raymond Crittenden and Archie Harris got Armstrong into scoring position. A run by

Armstrong's Ray Crittenden carries the ball in the 1943 Classic. *1944* Armstrong Rabza.

Crittenden broke the Walker goal line, but the play was called back, and the first half ended with the score still 6–0 in Walker's favor.

The third period picked up where the second had ended, with Armstrong controlling momentum. The Wildcats finally got on the scoreboard when Harris scored from the one, but the game remained tied as his ensuing run for the PAT was stopped short.

The remainder of the contest was Armstrong getting opportunities to score and the Walker defense coming up strong each time.

After the play that tied the game, the Dragons fumbled the kickoff, and the Wildcats recovered at the twenty-eight. But four plays only gained eight yards to the twenty, and Maggie Walker took over on downs.

The next chance came when the Wildcats intercepted a pass at the Dragons' twenty-nine. After being unable to move the ball, Armstrong pinned Walker deep when Crittenden punted the ball to the one-yard line.

Before the final gun, the Wildcats reached the Walker twenty-nine, but Ben Whaley intercepted Warren Hubbard's pass at the ten, and the game ended tied at 6–6.

Armstrong	0	0	6	0	**6**
Maggie Walker	6	0	0	0	**6**

W: Truman three-yard run (Blount run failed)
A: Harris one-yard run (Harris run failed)

THE WILDCATS STOPPED

November 24, 1944

The news on Saturday, November 24, 1944, was upbeat as the headlines of the *Times-Dispatch* reported that Allied patrols had crossed the Rhine and a massive air raid was successful over Japan.

The weather was expected to be cool and clear, and ten thousand fans were preparing to gather for a Classic meeting between an undefeated Armstrong and a once beaten Maggie Walker.

The opening period was pivotal as the Green Dragons hit early to get the Wildcats back on their heels. On the third play, Armstrong fumbled, and Walter Benjamin recovered for the Dragons at the Wildcats' thirty.

With Perry Briggs and Raymond Ross doing the bulk of the work, the Dragons moved the ball to the four. Briggs, the Walker quarterback, called his own number and ran over for the touchdown. Whit Graves tossed the conversion pass to Oliver Martin, and the Dragons led 7–0.

On the Wildcats' ensuing possession, Henry Wiggins dropped back to punt, but the kick was blocked by the charging Dragons, giving Walker the ball at the Armstrong forty-two.

With Ross and Briggs once again ripping through the Wildcat defense, the Dragons capped the drive when Ross scored, and Walker ended the opening period with a 13–0 advantage.

After two scoreless quarters, the Dragons' defense came up strong a third time when Swinson recovered Tom Barrett's fumble at the Armstrong forty. That drive ended with Briggs scoring his second touchdown of the game and Graves kicking the PAT to give the Dragons a 20–0 win.

Maggie Walker	13	0	0	7	**20**
Armstrong	0	0	0	0	**0**

W: Briggs four-yard run (Martin pass from Graves)
W: Ross run (PAT failed)
W: Briggs run (Graves kick)

And the Rout Was On

November 24, 1945

World War II was finally over. Young men were coming home, and many people in Richmond—fifteen thousand, in fact—gathered on a cold November 24 at City Stadium to watch the eighth Walker-Armstrong matchup. The Dragons were heavily favored, entering the game 5-1-0, while the Wildcats were 3-3-1. But no one expected to see what Walker quarterback Perry Briggs was about to do.

After forcing Armstrong to punt the ball early in the opening period, Walker used a twenty-three-yard run by Frank Mitchell to reach the Wildcat twenty-two, but a penalty killed the drive, and Briggs's thirty-yard punt pinned the Wildcats back at their own twelve.

Milton Smith blocked a second Armstrong punt, and the Dragons recovered the ball inside the Wildcats' ten. After moving the ball to the two-yard line, Briggs went over for the score, and his conversion pass to Ferney Green gave the Dragons a 7–0 advantage.

Regaining possession at their own forty-four, the Dragons drove to the Wildcat twenty-seven as the period ended.

In the second quarter, Maggie Walker moved the ball to the Armstrong three but was stopped on downs.

Hoping to catch the Walker defense off guard, Armstrong quarterback Melvin Stokes went to the air, but his pass was intercepted at the thirty by Daniel Branch, who returned it to the Wildcat twenty-one.

After being dropped for a four-yard loss back to the twenty-five, Briggs hit Green in stride at the ten, and the play went into the end zone to put the Dragons up 13–0.

Action from the 1945 Classic won by Maggie Walker 31–0. *1946* Armstrong Rabza.

With the clock running down, the Wildcats tried to get back in the game, only to have Mitchell step up for the interception of Stokes's pass and return the ball to the Armstrong forty-eight.

Branch moved the ball to the thirty-five. Several plays later, Oliver Martin pulled in a twelve-yard pass from Briggs that placed the ball on the Armstrong twenty-one.

Briggs then tossed a completion to Green that reached the seven. After the officials spotted the ball, Briggs passed to Martin, who was open in the end zone. The pass fell incomplete, but the clock did stop, and the Dragons had time for one final shot.

With fifteen thousand standing spectators looking on, Briggs brought the Dragons to the line and barked out the signals. With the snap of the ball, the Walker quarterback faded back, scanned the field, spotted Branch open and lofted the ball in his direction. Branch pulled the pass in and ended up in the Armstrong end zone for the score.

The attempted extra point came up short, but as the clock finally ran out and the teams headed for the locker rooms, the scoreboard read Walker 19, Armstrong 0.

Up by three touchdowns as the second half began, it would be the Maggie Walker defense that dominated the remainder of the contest.

In the third period, the Green Dragons pounced on a Wildcat fumble at the Armstrong twenty-eight and quickly advanced the ball to the Wildcat six.

Perry Briggs then tossed a six-yard touchdown pass to Bernard Potts, and as quick as that the Green Dragons were up 25–0. The Briggs-Potts combo completed the extra point pass for a 26–0 advantage.

As the period wrapped up, Armstrong finally showed signs of life as the Wildcats began to run weak side reverses and advanced to the Walker ten before turning the ball over on downs.

With the Armstrong offense spent, the Walker defense had one final thrill for the fans.

Briggs got in on a pass catch. Unfortunately for the Wildcats, it was an interception of a Stokes attempt that placed the ball at the Walker forty-one.

The Green Dragons drove the ball to the Armstrong twenty-five, where Briggs completed his fourth touchdown pass of the game, a twenty-five-yard toss to Potts. The duo then added the extra point, and the Dragons wrapped up the most one-sided win in the eight-year series with a 33–0 final score.

Maggie Walker	7	12	7	7	**33**
Armstrong	0	0	0	0	**0**

W: Briggs two-yard run (Green pass from Briggs)
W: Green twenty-five-yard pass from Briggs (PAT failed)
W: Branch seven-yard pass from Briggs (PAT failed)
W: Potts six-yard pass from Briggs (Potts pass from Briggs)
W: Martin twenty-five-yard pass from Briggs (Potts pass from Briggs)

NO WINNER, BUT STILL AN UPSET

November 30, 1946

Under a clear and warm sky, Armstrong and Maggie Walker felt each other out in the opening period as neither team threatened or moved the ball consistently. The period ended with the score tied at 0–0.

After the teams had switched ends of the field, Walker was on offense when a hooking penalty pushed the Dragons back to their own eight. Opting to get the ball out and away from the shadow of their own goal, the Dragons punted the ball, but it only traveled twenty-nine yards to the thirty-seven.

Setting up as the ball came down, Armstrong returned the kick seven yards to the thirty.

Back-to-back passes from Melvin Stokes to Guy Buster moved the ball to the Dragons' nine, giving the Wildcats a fresh set of downs.

Three rushing plays by Stokes gained just two yards, and Armstrong faced a fourth and goal at the seven. As the teams lined up and the play began, a yellow flag hit the ground, and Walker was found to have lined up offsides.

After the ball was walked off five yards to the two, the Wildcats once again lined up. This time, Stokes plunged over left tackle into the end zone, giving the Wildcats a 6–0 lead.

Setting up for the extra point, Stokes faded back and tossed the ball toward Charles Poole. But Bernard Potts reached in and knocked the ball away in the end zone for an incompletion.

On the ensuing set of downs, Walker started on its own thirty-four and proceeded to move the ball seventy-one yards to Armstrong's three. But the Wildcats' defense held, forcing the Dragons to give up possession on downs.

Ed Wood came on for Armstrong and punted the ball away. The half ended with the Wildcats up 6–0.

Halfway through the third period, Maggie Walker took over possession at its own thirty-four.

On first down, Potts tossed an eleven-yard pass to Furney Green, who moved the ball to the forty-five. Perry Briggs then called his own number and went twenty-yards on a left-end sweep that reached the Armstrong thirty-five before he was pushed out of bounds by Stokes.

On the next play, Briggs went around the right end for a sixteen-yard gain to the nineteen. On first down, Potts gained four to the fifteen, and on second, Briggs added six to the nine but was still just inches short of the first down.

Briggs was dropped by Charles Poole for a two-yard loss while attempting an end sweep on third down and faced a fourth and goal at the eleven as the period ended.

As the fans, numbering eighteen thousand, watched from both sides of the stadium, Briggs faded back and tossed an eleven-yard scoring pass to a wide-open Earl Randolph to tie the score 6–6.

The Dragons then lined up for the point-after attempt. Briggs tried to get a pass off to Green, but his toss wobbled and was knocked down by Stokes. The score remained tied.

Neither team threatened for the contest, and the series lead was still in Walker's camp. For all the yelling, cheering and sweating, the Classic had no winner, and both schools had to wait for next year.

Maggie Walker	0	0	0	6	**6**
Armstrong	0	6	0	0	**6**

A: Stokes two-yard run (pass failed)
W: Randolph eleven-yard pass from Briggs (pass failed)

A STATE CHAMPION (ACT ONE)

November 22, 1947

When the city of Richmond woke on November 22, 1947, it was greeted with the news that an expected meat shortage would last well into 1948. When people looked out the window, clouds threatened. Soon, rain would start to fall, and the temperature would not get out of the forties.

Still, a crowd of seventeen thousand made its way to City Stadium to see if a 6-0-1 Armstrong squad could capture the state VIAL championship by defeating Maggie Walker for the first time since 1941 or if the Dragons, at 3-3-1, could pull off a second straight upset.

In the opening period, both teams were battling jitters and a wet field as much as each other. On the opening kickoff, the Wildcats fumbled as Sam Stevenson recovered John D. Williams's misplay on the reception at the Armstrong thirty.

Two plays later, Walker's Earl Randolph lost control of the ball, and Armstrong's Donald Mask recovered at his own thirty-two.

With Williams and Melvin Stokes alternating carries, the Wildcats put together a drive that went sixty-seven yards to the Dragon one. Driving in for the score, Dan Austin lost control of the ball, which was recovered back at the six by Stevenson.

After Horace Hockaday got off a fifty-three-yard punt for the Dragons that ended up at the Wildcat forty-one, Armstrong staged its second straight drive, moving the ball to the twenty-nine before three straight major penalties pushed the Wildcats back to their own twenty-nine as the quarter ended.

The 1947 Armstrong Wildcat football team (state VIAL champions). *1948* Armstrong Rabza.

The second quarter quickly settled into a battle for field position, with little offense to show for any effort to move the ball; that is, until the clock was running out with the Wildcats on their own forty-one. Hoping to pin the Dragons deep, Alex Wood attempted to get off a punt on third down. But Charles Brown broke through and dropped Wood for a fifteen-yard loss back to the twenty-six.

Armstrong lined up for a fourth down attempt to kick the ball away, but for the second straight play, the Walker defense stood up as tackle Jasper Wilson nailed Wood for a nine-yard loss to the seventeen, giving the Dragons the ball at the Wildcats' goal as the half was nearing an end.

Hockaday and Wilbert Wilson pounded the line on four straight plays that gained eight yards as the Dragons came up two yards short of a first down at the nine as time ran out.

After twenty-four minutes, Armstrong had recorded eleven first downs and amassed 125 yards. Walker had a total of nine yards, all on the ground, and zero first downs. But neither team had lit up the scoreboard.

After a futile and frustrating half against a weaker foe, the Wildcats woke up in the third period.

Two minutes after the second half had begun, the Wildcats, with the ball at their own forty-eight, pulled out of the huddle and moved to the line of scrimmage. On defense, the Dragons had opted to over shift their defensive line to stop the gains that Stokes had ripped off in the first half.

Seeing what the Walker defense was doing, Armstrong went for a double reverse that ended up in the hands of Hobbs.

Fifty-five yards later, Hobbs was finally pulled down at the Walker seven, and the Wildcat fans sensed that Armstrong had gotten a handle on the game.

On first down, the Wildcats went to the double reverse a second time, and Stokes sped into the end zone untouched for the score. He followed his run with an extra point dash, and Armstrong was up 7–0.

During the ensuing series, it was the Wildcat defense that took control and, after forcing Hockaday to get off a punt that traveled just two yards, gave the offense the ball back at the Walker thirty-four.

That was when the Wildcats returned to the reverse. Andrew Hobbs got the ball and swept around the end for a thirty-one-yard touchdown. The attempt for the extra point failed, but with just five and a half minutes gone in the quarter, Armstrong had turned a 0–0 tie into a 13–0 advantage.

Early in the final quarter, Frank Peace, a 150-pound guard for the Wildcats, blocked Courtney Ridley's punt deep in the Walker end of the field. Charles Poole picked up the ball at the four and ran in to make the score 19–0.

The remainder of the game was marked by the Wildcats' domination of the Dragons on a field that was turned into mud.

When the tenth Classic ended, the Wildcats had held the Dragons to a total of just 23 yards, all on the ground, and no first downs. After a slow start, Armstrong finished with 301 yards, 268 on the ground, and rolled up fourteen first downs. Melvin Stokes proved his leadership, rushing the ball twenty-one times for 105 yards, and completed his lone pass attempt, a 33-yard toss to John D. Williams.

The win secured the Wildcats an undefeated season, the Virginia Interscholastic Athletic League State Championship and their first Classic title since 1941.

Armstrong	0	0	13	6	**19**
Maggie Walker	0	0	0	0	**0**

A: Stokes seven-yard run (Stokes run)
A: Hobbs thirty-one-yard run (PAT failed)
A: Poole blocked punt recovered in end zone (PAT failed)

Timeline Timeout

During the days of strict segregation, the African American schools in Virginia were organized under the umbrella of the Virginia Interscholastic Athletic League, later shortened to the Virginia Interscholastic Association (VIA). The counterpart to the white Virginia High School League, the VIA oversaw all aspects of athletic and forensic competition of its members.

Handcuffed by legally sanctioned inferior funding, the VIA still managed to provide district play, game officials and state champions at several levels. Along with Maggie Walker and Armstrong, Group I (largest schools) teams included Peabody-Petersburg, Burley-Charlottesville, I.C. Norcum-Portsmouth, Huntington-Newport News, Booker T. Washington-Norfolk, Carver-Chesapeake and Parker-Gray of Alexandria.

Other members of the VIA in the Richmond area were Virginia Randolph-Henrico County, Carver-Chesterfield County, John Gandy-Hanover County and Woodson-Hopewell.

Topping Twenty Thousand

November 27, 1948

The final Saturday of November in 1948 was a surprisingly warm sunny day. Twenty thousand fans gathered at City Stadium to watch a 4-2-1 Armstrong squad meet arch-rival Maggie Walker, which entered the eleventh annual Classic 8-2-0.

Despite the sun, the playing field was muddy after earlier rains and several games having been played over previous days.

In the opening period, both teams were able to move the ball, but it wasn't until the squads had exchanged punts that the first break occurred.

After Wildcat Sammy Thompson received a Courtney Ridley punt at his own twenty-five, Leon Robertson lost the handle on first down, and Sam Stevenson recovered the ball at the six.

On third and goal at the three, Charles Williams, playing in his final Classic, bulled over for the score to the delight of the Dragon faithful.

Up 6–0, Walker appeared to have added the extra point on Stevenson's run, but the Dragons were flagged for motion and on the second attempt came up short. The score remained 6–0.

The second period opened with Armstrong on the move, driving to the Walker twenty-seven off a play that saw guard Mike Green take the handoff and lateral to Ed Wood. On the ensuing play, Williams intercepted a Wildcat pass and returned the ball to his own forty-five.

Carroll Mosby gained fifteen, but the Wildcats stiffened, forcing the Green Dragons to punt.

After Thompson misplayed Ridley's kick, the Green Dragons got a golden opportunity to add to their advantage when end Charles Brown recovered the ball at the Armstrong ten.

On first down, however, Walker was penalized fifteen-yards for clipping and faced first and goal at the twenty-five. A short pass from Williams to Billy Wertz moved the ball to the twenty, but Armstrong held and took over on downs.

With neither team threatening again, the first half ended with Walker up 6–0.

The third period was nothing but a punting duel as both squads booted the ball three times each. In fact, the final quarter started with Wood pinning the Dragons back at their nine.

Unable to generate any offense, Walker attempted to kick the ball out, but it traveled to the Green Dragons' twenty-seven, giving the Wildcats their best field possession of the afternoon.

As the fans in the stands began to lean forward, the Armstrong offense broke the huddle and lined up over the ball. As Robertson carried the ball, it was the Armstrong faithful who roared when the Wildcat halfback headed around the Walker right end and rumbled to the fourteen.

On the ensuing play, Walker was flagged offsides, and Robertson's next run placed the ball on the seven. Faced with third and goal, the Wildcats called a double reverse that ended up in the hands of Sammy Thompson.

Thompson broke free and, with the blue and orange on the field and in the stands shouting their approval, crossed the goal line to tie the game at 6–6 with ten minutes and forty seconds left in the game. William Powell took the ball and ran in for the extra point; suddenly, Armstrong was up 7–6.

The rest of the game returned to a showcase for the punters, and the clock ran out with Wildcats at the Dragon twenty-six. In the contest, eighteen total punts were kicked, nine apiece by both teams.

Armstrong	0	0	0	7	**7**
Maggie Walker	6	0	0	0	**6**

W: Williams three-yard run (run failed)
A: Thompson seven-yard run (Powell run)

EVERYTHING BUT POINTS

November 26, 1949

A day after the final streetcar clanged its way along the tracks in Richmond, the Armstrong–Maggie Walker Classic turned twelve years old. With a predicted fifteen thousand to attend the game, the teams were deemed equal in ability—even though Armstrong's record of 4-1-2 was better than Walker's 6-3-0.

Timeline Timeout

Just two years had passed since Jackie Robinson broke the invisible, but apparently unbreakable, color barrier in Major League Baseball. On September 30, 1949, the Richmond Rebels, members of the semiprofessional American Football League (AFL), made an even more daring, if unnoticed, move.

Frederick "Cannonball" Cooper, who had been on the staff at Maggie Walker as an assistant coach since 1947, signed a contract to play for the Rebels and became the first African American to play professionally in the South.

Cooper, from Haddonfield, New Jersey, attended Virginia Union University (VUU) in 1940 and won immediate success for the Panthers before sitting out the 1941 season with an injury. He starred again in 1942. But World War II called, and for the 1943–44 seasons he was with the Third Army in Europe. He returned to finished at VUU and began teaching history at Maggie Walker in 1947 while serving as an assistant coach to "Stretch" Gardner.

In 1948, Cooper played for the Atlantic City, New Jersey Reds in an exhibition game against the Rebels. He so impressed Rebel owner Harry C. Seibold that he was offered a contract for the '49 season.

The results were impressive: Cooper led the league in yards rushed (gaining 665 yards) and touchdowns scored (ten in ninety-five carries). As a result, the Rebels won the AFL championship.

Walls that still stood off the field were breaking down on the gridiron.

One key was that both teams entered the game with hurt leaders. Armstrong sophomore tailback Leon Robertson was recovering from an ankle injury and would be spelled by freshmen Roscoe Gibson and Wallace Munford.

For the Dragons, running back John Cunningham was sidelined with a broken arm but would try to play with the injury heavily taped. He would be replaced by freshman John Hairston, who joined quarterback Carroll Mosby in the backfield.

The biggest change was not on the field, however, but on the sideline, as John "Pop" Williams took over as the Walker coach from Arthur Gardner.

With the crowd exceeding nineteen thousand and the temperature in the mid-forties, the contest opened with the teams exchanging punts. On the game's third possession, the snap from center sailed over Wildcat punter Bill Whaley's head, and the Dragons recovered at the Armstrong twenty-seven.

The Armstrong defense held, and the remainder of the first quarter was a punting duel between Armstrong's Whaley and Walker's Isaac Bowles.

As the half was ticking down, the Green Dragons got another shot at the Wildcat end zone. With ball at the Walker forty-two, Titus Tillman connected on a forty-one-yard pass to John Oliver that placed the ball on the Armstrong seventeen with just seventeen seconds left before intermission. The Dragons rushed to the line and got off a play as the clock ran out. Tillman took a long lateral and broke free into the Armstrong end zone for a touchdown. But the Walker celebration on the field and in the stands ended as a yellow flag lay on the ground back at the line of scrimmage. The Dragons, in their rush to get the play off, were caught for illegal procedure, and the half ended with neither team putting a point on the scoreboard.

The second half was spent between the twenty yard lines as both teams moved the ball but neither took advantage of any opportunities given by the other.

As time was running out, Walker opted to protect the ball, and the Dragons stayed on the ground. Mosby was dropped for a six-yard loss back at the ten, and on the next play, Hairston lost his handle on the ball. The Wildcats recovered at the ten for one last desperate chance to score.

Lining up for first down with nineteen thousand pairs of eyes glued on both the field and the clock, Armstrong gained one yard to the nine on Robertson's first down run. But the next three plays, all pass attempts, failed to find receivers. The Armstrong faithful watched in disappointment as the Wildcats came up empty and the Green Dragons regained possession.

Carroll Mosby gained nine yards out to the nineteen, and then, on second and one, the Walker workhorse gained another eleven yards to the thirty. Sensing a slim chance of hope that one broken play might go all the way, Walker went to the air. But just as the Wildcats had done on the previous series, the Dragons failed to connect on three straight passes. As the final gun sounded, Bowles punted the ball harmlessly away.

As the teams left the field and the Tishman Trophy went unclaimed, two outstanding performances had been overshadowed. Walker's Mosby finished the game with 111 yards on twenty-five carries, and William Powell rushed the ball twenty-one times, gaining 69 yards for the Wildcats.

SECTION II

Second Quarter

(1950–1959)

Snow on the Field, Fires in the Stands

November 25, 1950

November 25, 1950, found the United States at war again, this time in Korea. As people scanned the front page of the *Richmond Times-Dispatch*, the United Nations force that had pushed toward the Chinese border faced a major Communist counterattack head on.

Back home in Richmond, the major news item was that the thirteenth Armstrong–Maggie Walker would kickoff at 2:00 p.m. before an anticipated crowd of seventeen thousand. Walker entered the game the favorite, sporting a 7-2-0 record compared to Armstrong's 4-3-0.

But those who looked out their windows or stepped out the front door could see and feel the snowstorm that was about to begin. By the time the captains met at midfield for the coin toss, the wind had already started to pick up, the field at City Stadium was dusted with snow and the temperature was in the low twenties. And that was the best the weather would get.

With just 10,500 paid spectators braving the elements, the opening period saw Armstrong with the wind at its back, and the Wildcats took full advantage. Punter George Burke got off several punts that kept the more powerful Dragons deep in their own end of the gridiron. Field conditions were nullifying Walker's superior ground game as star running back John Cunningham was held to a minus seven yards on four carries.

The 1950 Armstrong coaching staff. *From left to right*: Ulis Shelton, Maxie Robinson and Anthony James. *1951* Armstrong Rabza.

It was the underdog Wildcats who threatened first as Walker punter Isaac Bowles's fourth down kick into the wind traveled just ten yards to the Dragon twenty-nine. With Howard Reynolds and William Powell doing the rushing, the Wildcats drove to the Walker two before the Dragon defense stiffened. On fourth and goal, Powell tossed the game's first pass and connected with Rudy McCann. But the Dragons read the play perfectly and dropped him for a three-yard loss as the first quarter ended with Walker regaining possession on its own six.

With the wind now at their back, the Green Dragons opted to kick the ball away rather than risk a turnover in the shadows of their own goal post.

The play turned out perfectly. With a combination of Bowles's leg and a strong wind, the ball sailed sixty-four yards to the Armstrong thirty for a major switch in field position.

After yet another exchange of punts, the half ended scoreless.

With conditions preventing any halftime entertainment, the crowd, whose number had been cut in half, began to light small fires in the stands to stay warm. Stadium security quickly put a stop to that.

The second half started with Armstrong in possession, and Wallace Munford got off the longest run of the contest, a thirteen-yard dash. Held on downs, the Wildcats attempted to get the ball away, but Burke's punt, through a combination of a stiff wind and a bad bounce, covered a net of minus two yards.

Several possessions later, with the clock running down on the third quarter, Maggie Walker was in possession at the Wildcat forty-seven, determined to move the ball as far as possible with the wind at its back. A first down pass from Henry Lee to Cunningham fell incomplete. On the next play, Cunningham broke free for ten yards to give the Dragons their initial first down of the contest.

On third and nine at the Armstrong thirty-six, Lee tossed a fourteen-yard pass to Bowles that advanced the ball to the twenty-two as the period ended.

Now moving into the wind, the Dragons kept the ball on the ground, and on first down, Earl Russell gained one yard to the Wildcat twenty-one. Cunningham then ran a delayed sweep around end for eight yards to the thirteen. Russell got the ball on third down and gained one, but when the chains were brought out, the ball was just short of the first down marker.

Needing just inches, Walker got yards—eight to be exact—as Cunningham ripped through the Armstrong defense for a run to the five, giving the Dragons four more downs.

Sticking with Cunningham, the Green Dragons' backfield leader got one yard, to the four, but was pushed back one on second down. Facing a third and goal at the five, Cunningham took the ball, pulled up short and attempted a jump pass to James Harrison that fell incomplete.

With several thousand shivering fans still in the stands cheering for a score or a defensive stand, the Green Dragons broke the huddle and came to the line. The ball ended up in Cunningham's hands, and he broke to the left for an end sweep. Five yards later, he was in the end zone, and the scoreless tie was broken.

Russell ran in the extra point, but the play was called back as the Dragons were called for motion in the backfield. On a second attempt, Lee flipped a pass to Bowles that fell harmlessly to the ground, but Walker was up 6–0.

With only about three thousand fans, mostly rooting for Walker, left in the stands, the game ended on the longest play from scrimmage. Calvin Rivers tossed a pass to McCann that covered thirty-eight yards before being stopped at the Walker forty-four.

Maggie Walker	0	0	0	6	**6**
Armstrong	0	0	0	0	**0**

W: Cunningham five-yard run (pass failed)

A State Champion (Act Two)

November 24, 1951

One game. That was all Maggie Walker had to face in a dream that had started back in September and now was to end on a sloppy, wet City Stadium field on November 24, 1951. After steamrolling nine straight foes by a combined score of 332–6, the Green Dragons were one game away from a perfect season and the VIA State Championship.

But that one game was against arch-rival Armstrong, and there could be nothing sweeter for the Wildcats (5-2-0) than to derail the Green Dragons and win the Classic championship for the first time since 1948.

When the city of Richmond woke that morning, overcast skies and the threat of rain provided the orange and blue with the great equalizer: poor playing conditions.

With a crowd of twelve thousand in the stands, the rain began. After stopping the Wildcats on the game's opening series, the Dragons' first play from scrimmage was a handoff to John Cunningham, the team's mainstay. Cunningham, a senior, had rushed for 1,117 yards in the first nine games and added 8 on this carry.

But from that point, the game turned into a case of the Green Dragons' offense crashing into a Wildcat defense that gave but refused to break. Aided by penalties and a fumble recovered by Ed Wood, Armstrong survived the first quarter in a scoreless tie.

The opening of the second quarter found Walker facing a third and fourteen at the Wildcat twenty-six. Dragon halfback Isaac Bowles fooled the Wildcat defense when he pulled up short and tossed a pass to Hamlin Mason in the end zone for the touchdown Walker hoped would open up the game.

Cheers turned to groans when fans noticed that back near the line of scrimmage, a yellow flag lay in the mud. Backfield in motion, Maggie Walker.

The touchdown was nullified, and two plays later, Bowles punted to the Wildcat seven.

Getting the ball right back, Walker appeared to have reached the Armstrong thirteen when John Holmes broke free on a fifteen-yard run. But the play was nullified, as the Dragons were caught offsides and the drive came up short.

With time running out in the half, the Dragons got one more shot at the end zone.

A second down pass from Bowles to Milton McLaughlin gave Walker the ball at the Wildcat nine, with just seconds left on the clock. Luther White's pass was incomplete, but it did stop the clock to allow one final play.

With all twelve thousand faces in the stands, most under umbrellas, watching, Bowles flipped the ball to Cunningham standing alone in the end zone. All twelve thousand stood in stunned silence—half in shock, the other half in relief—as he dropped the ball, and the half ended scoreless.

After an uneventful third quarter, the game entered the final period, still a scoreless deadlock.

A Walker drive that reached the Armstrong forty-seven was halted when Charles Porter intercepted Bowles at his own twenty-two. After runs by John Smith and Calvin Taylor moved the ball to the twenty-eight, Taylor appeared to move the chains with a critical four-yard run, but the play was wiped out by an offside penalty. Bill Whaley backed up to punt, but as the ball was snapped, Joe Nixon and Willie Clegg broke free to smother the ball at the thirteen.

On first down, Cunningham took the handoff and ran past and over most of the Armstrong defense into the end zone. This time, no yellow flags were thrown, and the touchdown stood. The run for the conversion point failed, but after three quarters of frustration, Maggie Walker owned a 6–0 advantage with just over nine minutes to play.

Armstrong made one last push as Andy Rivers connected with Smith on a twenty-two-yard pass that reached the Walker forty-five. But the next toss was intercepted by James Harrison. The rest of the game was a matter of the Dragons running out the clock.

With the win, the Dragons claimed their second straight Classic title, their first ever 10-0-0 record and the VIAL State Championship.

Maggie Walker	0	0	0	6	**6**
Armstrong	0	0	0	0	**0**

W: Cunningham thirteen-yard run (run failed)

MAXIE'S BEST

November 29, 1952

While the war in Korea seemed to show no change, in Richmond, changes in the Classic contest held on November 29 were definite.

The first was the opening of a new building for Armstrong High. After thirty-one years at Prentis and Leigh Street, a new facility was built at Thirty-first Street on Church Hill and occupied in September. Second, after two years of playing in the shadow of Maggie Walker, Armstrong's football team had come of age. The Wildcats had won five games but weren't in the VIA title picture because of a 13–12 loss to Booker T. Washington of Norfolk.

The defending state champion Dragons were young, but Coach Williams had led them to an 8-1-0 record, despite having lost nine of eleven starters from the 1951 squad.

The weather for the fifteenth meeting of Armstrong and Maggie Walker was cold and raw, but for the first time in three years, the sky was clear. These conditions brought out fourteen thousand spectators, the largest crowd since 1949, expecting to see yet another tight contest.

The Wildcats, hungry after three years of coming up empty against the Dragons, struck early. After recovering a Walker fumble at the Dragon

Top: Thirty-first Street, site of Armstrong High School, 1952–2004. *1953* Armstrong Rabza.

Bottom: Armstrong students visit the construction site of the new Armstrong High located on Thirty-first Street. *1953* Armstrong Rabza.

thirty-nine, Armstrong moved the ball to the nine on an eight-yard run by Bill Whaley and a twenty-two-yard pass from Whaley to Jackson Rozier. On third and goal at the nine, Wildcat quarterback Howard Reynolds tossed the ball to John Quarles, who made a circus catch and got both feet down in the end zone for the first Armstrong points since 1948. Clarence Hicks booted the extra point, and the Wildcats were up 7–0 as the opening quarter ended.

On the ensuing kickoff, Milton McLaughlin returned the ball to the Walker thirty-six.

Eight plays later, the Dragons were at the Armstrong seven. Tailback Luther White took the ball and, rather than rush forward, faded back and passed to a diving Al Johnson, who caught the ball in the end zone to pull the Dragons to 7–6. Thomas Johnson ran in the conversion, and the score was tied at 7–7.

The Wildcats opted to discard the *T*-formation for a full-power right that placed the entire Wildcat backfield in the position to block for Reynolds. Four plays moved the ball to the Walker forty-three, where Reynolds once again took the snap.

After cutting off behind the right tackle, the Wildcats' quarterback edged down the sideline for several yards and then cut back toward the center of the field.

As White, who doubled as the Dragons' safety, came up for the tackle, Reynolds sidestepped him and broke into the open field for a forty-three-yard scoring run.

Hicks booted his second extra point, and the Wildcats took a 14–7 advantage as the second quarter ended and the teams headed to the locker rooms.

The Wildcats opened the second half on defense, but not for long, as Thomas Bullock intercepted a Dragon pass and returned the ball to the Walker twenty-seven.

Runs by Leonardo Chappelle and Whaley moved the ball to the six. Whaley covered the final six yards on the ground, and Hicks's PAT gave Armstrong a 21–7 advantage.

Dominating the Dragons on defense, the Wildcats used that defense to put the game out of reach early in the final period.

As the Dragons attempted to punt from their twenty-one, Van Whaley, Albert Thomas and Ed Wood broke through to hit Thomas Johnson before he could get the kick off, and Whaley recovered the ball at the three.

Two plays later, with the ball at the one, Charles Porter got the call and bulled over for the score. Hicks missed the PAT, but the Wildcats owned a 27–7 lead, and the Armstrong defense stifled the Dragons for the remainder of the game. The team that Maxie Robinson said was his best ever gave a strong showing to support that claim.

When the final gun sounded, the Wildcats once again were Classic champs. Armstrong rolled up 316 yards of offense, 276 coming on the ground. Whaley led the onslaught, gaining 74 yards on eighteen carries. Chappelle added 56 yards; Reynolds, 26; Jimmy Herring, 44; and Porter, 36.

Walker's season of 8-2-0 would always be remembered as the one in which it lost the Classic. The Dragons were held to just 40 yards on the ground, but White completed eight of twenty-three passes for 110 yards.

Armstrong	7	7	7	6	**27**
Maggie Walker	0	7	0	0	**7**

A: Quarles nine-yard pass from Reynolds (Hicks kick)
W: A. Johnson seven-yard pass from White (T. Johnson run)
A: Reynolds forty-three-yard run (Hicks kick)
A: W. Whaley six-yard run (Hicks kick)
A: Porter one-yard run (kick failed)

Don't Believe the Headlines

November 28, 1953

While the conflict in Korea had come to an unsteady truce in the summer, a new and closer battle reached the front page of the *Richmond Times-Dispatch* on the morning of November 28, 1953. United Sates Attorney General Brownell advised the Supreme Court that it was free to outlaw segregation in the nation's public school systems but declared that he favored a gradual transition. The war against segregation was on.

That afternoon, a war of a different kind was about to begin as the sixteenth annual Armstrong–Maggie Walker Classic was timed to kick off at 2:00 p.m. before eleven thousand spectators on a cold and cloudy, but dry, afternoon.

By all accounts, the Dragons were favored to recapture the Classic title, having gone 6-1-2 over the season with a shot at the state title, while the Wildcats, who hadn't played for three weeks, stood 2-2-1. At least, that's what the papers said.

To make the most of its one chance to play in November, Armstrong knew that it had to have a plan. That plan was to allow the Walker

The 1953 Armstrong Wildcat football team. *1954* Armstrong Rabza.

ground game to do what it could and concentrate on Dragon quarterback Luther White.

In the opening period, the Wildcats struck first when Jimmy Herring scored on a three-yard run. Charles Porter added the kick for an extra point, and Armstrong led 7–0.

In the second quarter, the Wildcats reached the Dragon thirty-three, where quarterback Moses Morrell pitched the ball to Andrew Rivers. Rivers pulled up and tossed a pass to Jackson Rozier, who had broken free downfield. The play ended with Rozier in the Walker end zone and the Wildcats up 13–0.

But then the game changed, and the Armstrong plan was tested for the rest of the contest.

In the third period, the Dragons blocked a Wildcat punt to take possession at the Armstrong twenty-one. White faked a pass and ran the ball to the three, setting up George Davis's burst across the goal line. White ran in the conversion, and suddenly Walker pulled to 13–7.

Getting the ball back at midfield, Walker drove to the fifteen before Ed Wood intercepted a White pass to end the threat.

As the quarter came to an end, Walker was on the move again as runs by Booker Cox and Waddell Brock moved the ball to the Armstrong eleven. But then Beauregard Evans caused a fumble, and Irvin McQueen recovered at the fifteen.

Sticking to its defensive scheme, which left only four men along the defensive line, the Wildcats allowed the Dragons to run the ball but stymied White as the clock began to wind down.

With three minutes and twenty seconds remaining, the Dragons made one last push as their dream of a second VIA state title in two years hung in the balance. Runs by Cox, Davis and Lewis Brown moved the ball to the Armstrong twenty with just thirty-five seconds left.

And then, for one final time, the plan worked. White was dropped for a four-yard loss, and with just two men rushing on the game's last play, the snap was misplayed, the ball rolled harmlessly back to the forty-four and Armstrong had its upset. That's what the papers said.

Armstrong	7	6	0	0	**13**
Maggie Walker	0	0	7	0	**7**

A: Herring three-yard run (Porter kick)
A: Rozier thirty-three-yard pass from Rivers (kick failed)
W: Davis two-yard run (White run)

Rain, Rain Go Away

November 20, 1954

When morning came to Richmond on November 20, 1954, the *Richmond Times-Dispatch* reported that a meeting of the state commission formed to study how Virginia would react to the Supreme Court's *Brown v. The Board of Education* (Topeka, Kansas) would be held on the upcoming Wednesday. The weather forecast called for fog in the morning and rain in the afternoon.

In the sports section, a brief prediction expected a crowd of ten thousand to attend the seventeenth Armstrong–Maggie Walker Classic that afternoon, the first pre-Thanksgiving meeting between the schools since 1947.

The predicted rain and fog welcomed the nine thousand fans who filed into City Stadium, but at least the temperature was a comfortable sixty degrees. The field was a soaked mess, and play would certainly be affected.

In the opening period, the teams slogged in the mud until Walker was forced to punt. The Wildcats misplayed the ball, and in the ensuing scramble, James Taylor came up with possession at the Walker thirty-eight.

Hoping to counter the less than pristine playing conditions, the Dragons lined up in a formation that placed both ends spread wide and ran Louis Collins, William Smith and Eddie Mayfield into the line. That strategy worked in getting Walker to the Armstrong thirty-six before the Wildcat defense stiffened, and as the period ended, the orange and blue held and gained possession.

As the field conditions worsened, the second quarter saw a single offensive push when Armstrong reached the Walker thirty-five before being pushed back to the forty-seven as the half ended scoreless.

While the second half saw more action than the first, nothing resulted in points.

After an exchange of punts in the third quarter, Armstrong got its best chance under the conditions. Irvin McQueen returned a short punt fifteen yards to the Walker thirty-three, and runs by Jimmy Herring, Walter Woodson and McQueen moved the ball nine yards to the twenty-four. Facing a fourth and one, quarterback Moses Norrell called his own number and gained four yards to the twenty, giving the Wildcats a new set of downs.

On the very next play, the ball came loose, and the Dragons recovered it on the sixteen.

A major penalty pushed Walker back to the one, and sophomore Samuel Barnes booted a fifty-nine-yard punt from out of the end zone to end Armstrong's best chance.

The final period continued much as the rest of the game had, until, pinned back at his own sixteen, Norrell got off a thirty-four-yard punt for the Wildcats that traveled to midfield.

Standing under the ball, William Smith took the kick and returned it eleven yards to the Armstrong thirty-nine.

On first down, Warren Smith was dropped for a four-yard loss back to the forty-three. Waddell Brock got three yards back on second down, and on third, Norvell Chambers tossed a pass that was caught by Eddie Mayfield covering nine yards to the thirty-one.

Facing a fourth and two, Brock got the ball and raced six yards around end to the twenty-five to move the chains and give the Dragons a fresh set of downs with six minutes remaining in the contest.

Back-to-back two-yard runs by Smith moved the ball to the twenty-one.

On third and six, a pass by Chambers fell incomplete. Going for it on fourth down, Brock carried the ball. However, Harvey Stewart broke free of his blocker, stuffed the play for a two-yard loss, ended the drive and gave the Wildcats the ball.

The few hardy fans who stayed to the end saw Armstrong survive being pinned deep in its own territory as the game ended as it had started—scoreless. In the end, all those who remained seemed happy to go home.

All You Need Is One Play

November 26, 1955

For the second straight year, the headline that greeted Richmond on the morning of Classic Saturday (as it was now called) was about the battle against segregation. The Interstate Commerce Commission upheld its ban on segregation for trains and buses that crossed state lines. Clearer battle lines were being drawn over the Jim Crow laws that still hung like a dark cloud over Virginia.

For those football fans in Richmond, the Armstrong-Walker showdown was back on the Saturday after Thanksgiving. Owning a 6-2-0 record, Maggie Walker needed a win over the Wildcats to grab a share of the VIA state title. Armstrong entered the game at 3-2-1 and was a one-touchdown underdog.

A crowd of fourteen thousand chilled fans (the temperature never got out of the thirties) watched as Armstrong kicked off to start the eighteenth Classic.

After the Armstrong defense stopped the Dragons, the Wildcats took over at their sixteen. Runs by Irvin McQueen, Tyrone McQueen and Tom Page moved the ball to the thirty-five before the drive died, and Theodore Spurlock punted the ball to the Walker forty-two.

On first down, Louis Brown broke free around end to gain sixteen yards to the Armstrong forty-two. With Brown and William Smith advancing the ball to the thirty-two, the Dragons fumbled a lateral that was recovered by Armstrong at its own forty-five.

In the second quarter, with the Wildcats set up to punt the ball away from their own end of the field, Franklin Lyons broke through to block the ball and recover it at the twenty-one.

On first down, Brown carried the ball eleven yards to the ten, and Smith gained three to the seven.

The Armstrong defense stiffened as two Brown runs moved the ball to the two. On fourth and goal, Brown got the call for the third play but was stopped short by William Pompey, Clyde Eldridge and Harvey Stewart.

With that failed drive, defense took over again, and as the half ended, the score was still—what else?—scoreless.

After the Dragon defense, led by Paul Hurdle, Joe Birchett, Alfred Payne and Edward Prince, handcuffed the Wildcats in the third period, Armstrong drove to the Walker twenty-two early in the fourth, only to turn the ball over on downs.

Pierce Callaham's first down pass fell incomplete. But on the ensuing play, he tossed a pass toward the right side of the line. Brown, coming out of the backfield, pulled in the ball at the Dragon's forty-four and turned upfield. Irvin McQueen came up for the tackle and grabbed a part of Brown's leg, but his grip fell short as Brown regained his balance and ran untouched the rest of the way for a seventy-eight-yard touchdown, the longest for Maggie Walker in the history of the Classic.

With everyone watching stunned, the Dragons were up 6–0 in just one toss of the ball. The green and white faithful roared, "Did you see that!" while the orange and blue moaned, "Did you see that?"

There was one last offensive threat of the afternoon, but it would have no influence on the outcome of the game.

As the clock wound down, Paul Botts intercepted a Wildcat pass at the Armstrong thirty-four and returned the ball nineteen yards to the fifteen.

The Dragons drove to the two, where the Wildcats held as the game came to an end. The Dragon faithful rushed the field and, in seconds, tore the goal post to the ground.

While the Dragons had been outgained (107 yards on the ground to 65), one pass competition, the game's lone pass completion, was the difference, and the 1955 Classic was in the books.

Maggie Walker	0	0	0	6	**6**
Armstrong	0	0	0	0	**0**

W: Louis Brown seventy-eight-yard pass from Pierce Callaham (PAT failed)

For Once, the Stats Told the Story

November 17, 1956

After eighteen meetings, eighteen marches first to Hovey Field and then City Stadium and eighteen halftime shows, neither Maggie Walker nor Armstrong could brag of being the Classic's best.

Both had won seven games, and five contests had ended in ties. But in 1956, the Dragons were the reigning title holders, having won 6–0 in 1955. They entered the second pre-Thanksgiving Day contest in three years as the favorite.

Running out of the winged *T*, Walker entered the game 4-2-0 and posted four shutouts, allowing just thirteen points. Armstrong was 3-3-0, utilizing the "Oklahoma *T*," which produced 1,327 yards, allowing quarterback Milton Marshall to set team records in passing yards for a game (107) and a season (265).

Classic number nineteen would be a battle between Walker's defense and Armstrong's offense. Would it end up in a sixth tie?

With just six thousand fans gathering to see the nineteenth Armstrong-Walker Classic in a cold, steady rain, the game started in a strangely perfect way as each team fumbled the ball on its respective first possession.

After the Dragons moved the ball to Armstrong's forty, the ball came loose and the Wildcats recovered.

On first down, running back William Grantham took a direct snap from center and ran thirteen yards to the Walker forty-seven. But a fumble was recovered by the Dragons, giving Walker a fresh set of downs.

Walker was unable to move the ball, and Bob Johnson punted it away to the Armstrong twenty-seven as the first period ended with neither team having anything but muddy uniforms to prove that a game was being played.

The second period got worse as the Wildcats had one play that involved a double fumble finally recovered by Elmer Dandridge.

For Walker, the lowlight was Johnson's high punt from his own forty-seven that landed, took a bizarre bounce backward and was called dead at the thirty-four for a minus thirteen yards.

After a halftime show by both bands that drew more applause than the action on the field, Armstrong kicked off. James Taylor pulled in the ball and raced twenty yards before being brought down at midfield.

Back-to-back runs by Eddie Mayfield advanced the ball five yards to the Wildcat forty-five, and on third down, Earl Nunnally rushed for seven yards to the thirty-eight to move the chains.

Sticking to its ground attack, Walker got a six-yard off-tackle run from Taylor, followed by a three-yard rush by Nunnally that left the Dragons one yard short of moving the chains. Taylor gained three, and the Dragons gained a fresh set of downs.

On the ensuing snap, Mayfield broke loose on an eleven-yard run for a first down at the fifteen. Taylor's run on the next snap covered seven yards to the eight as a soaked crowd stood to watch.

On second and three, Taylor got the first down on a four-yard run to the four. Then, with the lines taut for the surge that came on every play of every Classic game, Mayfield was given the ball. Four yards later, he crossed the goal, and the green and white on the field and in the stands roared as something other than the clock moved on the City Stadium scoreboard.

Walker went to the air for the conversion, but Johnson's pass to Welford Lewis was overthrown, and the Dragons held to a 6–0 advantage.

For the remainder of the contest, both teams struggled in the mud, and neither was ever threatened by the other. Walker out-gained Armstrong 127 yards to 59 and recorded eight first downs to one.

Maggie Walker	0	0	6	0	**6**
Armstrong	0	0	0	0	**0**

W: Mayfield four-yard run (pass failed)

Just for Kicks

November 30, 1957

When the sun rose on the morning of November 30, 1957, it came up behind a layer of clouds. But there was no call for rain, and when seven thousand spectators gathered at City Stadium for the twentieth renewal of the Armstrong–Maggie Walker Classic set to kick off at 2:00 p.m., the only problem was a muddy field.

Armstrong entered the game a slight favorite, sporting a 5-1-0 record, while Walker was at 5-4-0. Much to the chagrin of all on the field and in the stands, the rain did arrive, and playing conditions only worsened. The opening period was a sequence of fumbles, quick kicks and two dropped passes.

On the third play of the game, Armstrong fumbled, and Clem Watkins recovered at the Wildcat forty. After three running plays resulted in minus nine yards, Eugene Lewis punted to the Wildcat twenty-three, where the ball bounced off David Carter and was recovered by Walker's Julius Green.

Two plays later, Claude Duvall's pass to Ray Robbs was dropped behind the Armstrong defense at the seven, and the Dragons quick-kicked the ball away.

The Wildcats' chance came several plays later when Adolph Powell broke free from the Dragon coverage only to drop Monroe Beard's pass at the Walker forty.

The two punters, Powell for Armstrong and Lewis for Walker, exchanged kicks, and the opening period ended with the ball at the Wildcat one and the game scoreless.

The second quarter was, for those in the stands, too much of the same: Powell punt. Lewis punt. Wildcat fumble. Lewis punt.

But then, as rain pelted the field, the Wildcats began to stir. Behind the grinding running of Davis Carter and a thirteen-yard burst from William Grantham, Armstrong crossed midfield for the first time. An incomplete pass and fifteen-yard penalty later, however, the pattern picked up where it had left off.

Powell punted, and the first half ended with Walker at its thirty-eight.

For the entire second half, it was the punters, Powell and Lewis, who dominated play, keeping each other's team at bay. On one series in the third period, Lewis attempted a quick-kick on third down that was blocked. Recovering the loose ball, he promptly got off a fourth down punt that traveled thirty-four yards.

With just minutes left in the final period, Armstrong faced a fourth down at the Walker forty-six. Robbs intercepted Powell's pass attempt at the twenty-five. His return was stopped at midfield when he was tackled by Charles Bey.

The game ended shortly thereafter when Lewis recorded his lone completion of the contest, which Robbs took to the Armstrong thirty-nine before being stopped.

For the contest, there were more punts (twenty-one) than there were first downs (ten). There were more interceptions and fumble recoveries (four) than completed passes (two).

But the one thing that was lacking in every stat was points. There were none.

NO PICNIC, BUT STILL A WIN

November 22, 1958

As November 22 dawned, the morning papers reported that the whirlwind issue concerning desegregation of schools in Virginia was coming to a head. Eleven days earlier, the *Richmond Times-Dispatch* had reported that a local judge put off a decision to make a ruling over the city's refusal to admit six African American elementary students into two white schools.

That morning, the paper reported that State Attorney General A.S. Harrison claimed that the state constitution did not require Virginia to maintain statewide public schools. This would open the door for Governor James Almond's plan to close any school that allowed even one incident of integration.

For those preparing to attend the twenty-first Classic, it was the news on the weather page that was closely read. Cool and cloudy but no rain was a most welcome forecast, and by 2:00 p.m. fifteen thousand fans had gathered as Armstrong entered the game strongly favored with a 5-1-0 record that saw the Wildcats start with five straight shutouts before falling to B.T. Washington-Norfolk 14–6.

The Walker Dragons hoped an upset win in the game would improve on a 4-1-2 record that left the green and white idle for two weeks.

Any Armstrong fan who thought the game would be a picnic was jerked back to reality when Stuart Robinson recovered a Wildcat fumble at the orange and blue twenty-three early in the contest. With Ray Robbs and Berry Carter carrying the load, Walker drove to the twelve. On second down, Walter Carter took the handoff and ran around end for the score. Barry Carter kicked the PAT, and the Dragons went up 7–0.

The 1958 Armstrong Wildcat football team. *1959* Armstrong Rabza.

As the opening period came to an end, it was the Wildcats who struck as Billy McLean recovered a mishandled Dragon handoff at the Walker twenty-six.

In the opening minutes of the second quarter, David Carter carried five straight times to the two, and a sixth rush broke the goal line. Tom Capers booted the PAT, and suddenly the game was tied 7–7.

Before the intermission neared, Walker threatened and drove to the Armstrong nineteen. Walter Carter appeared to have made up for his earlier fumble with a nineteen-yard touchdown burst, but the Dragons were flagged for holding and the score was nullified.

Turned back, Walker had one more possession as the clock was running down, but the Dragons fumbled the ball at their own twenty-six as time ran out.

After the third period opened with an exchange of punts, Armstrong took over possession at its own forty. With quarterback Monroe Beard, Adolph Powell, Sam Gladden and George Wallace each carrying the ball, the Wildcats moved the ball to the twenty-two.

Beard took the snap and faked handoffs to Gladden and then Wallace before pitching out to McLean. McLean avoided the Dragon defenders closing in and, instead of being trapped behind the line of scrimmage, broke free around right end and scampered into the end zone for the score. Capers added the extra point, and Armstrong went up 14–7.

But the game was far from over, and on the ensuing kickoff, David Carter was injured and unable to return.

Maggie Walker, taking over at its own twenty-five, went to a single-wing formation that was over balanced, with only an end on one side of the center, and began to pick up some yardage as Robbs, both Carters and Willie Burney carried the load.

Moving to the Armstrong twenty-five, the Dragons fumbled the ball, and the Wildcats recovered at the twenty-three. Moments later, Walker got the ball back at its own forty-five and drove to the Wildcat one.

With the crowd of fifteen thousand on its feet and the Dragons facing fourth and goal, Walker got off the snap, but McLean and Bill Harris broke through the line and dropped the play back at the four as Armstrong held and regained possession.

In the final quarter, the Dragons had one final chance to tie the game and drove to the Wildcat twenty-three. Berry Carter faded back and tossed the ball toward the end zone, where Powell intercepted the pass at the five.

With the clock running out, Beard ran the ball into the line twice, and the Wildcats captured the Classic, 14–7.

Armstrong	0	7	7	0	**14**
Maggie Walker	7	0	0	0	**7**

W: W. Carter twelve-yard run (B. Carter kick)
A: D. Carter two-yard run (Capers kick)
A: McLean twenty-two-yard run (Capers kick)

THE DEFENSE RESTS

November 28, 1959

With neither team challenging for a state title, the twenty-second Classic was played for pride. After twenty-one meetings, the two rivals stood toe to toe, each with eight wins and five games tied. And there was nothing in the season records of the two rivals to indicate that either team held an edge over the other.

Maggie Walker entered the game with a 4-2-3 record, and Armstrong was 3-3-0. When ten thousand spectators gathered at City Stadium on a warm Saturday afternoon at the end of November, little in the way of fireworks were expected. What they got was a one-sided Fourth of July show.

The game opened in a way that in one sense reflected nothing of what the contest would become and in another reflected it all.

On the first possession, Walker fumbled, and Wildcat Richard Allen recovered at the Dragon twenty-six. Stanley Brown moved the ball to the fourteen before the Walker defense bucked up and took over on downs back at the twenty-one.

Walter Carter advanced the ball to the forty-three, where quarterback Joe Tisdale hit Allen Cole on the run for a fifty-seven-yard touchdown pass. The extra point failed, but the Dragons were up 6–0 as the game entered the second quarter.

Possessing the ball at the Armstrong forty-eight, Tisdale tossed passes to Cole and Willie Burney that moved the chains to the fourteen.

With the ball advanced to the Wildcats' nine, Carter got the call, and his eight-yard burst gave the Dragons a first and goal at the one. The Armstrong defense held for no gain, and the teams lined up a second time in the shadow of the Wildcat goal posts.

On second down, Tisdale called his own number and bulled over for the score. A second extra point attempt failed, and Walker went up 12–0.

The remainder of the period settled into a defensive struggle and the half ended; the Dragons headed to the locker rooms with a 12–0 lead and the Wildcats with a minus five yards of offense.

The second half opened with the Wildcats returning the kickoff back to their own twenty-five.

Trying to get something going, Brown tossed a screen pass that bounced off the intended receiver and was intercepted by Melvin Cowens at the line of scrimmage. With everybody heading the other way, Cowens ran untouched into the end zone, and before many in the stands had gotten back from the concessions, the Dragons led 18–0.

The defenses on both sides of the ball dominated the remainder of the third period as the Dragons entered the final twelve minutes holding a three-touchdown advantage.

Robert McKeever took over at quarterback for the Wildcats and moved Armstrong to its own forty, where he went to the air. The ball was picked off

The 1959 Armstrong cheerleaders. *1960* Armstrong Rabza.

at the line of scrimmage by Walker tackle Stuart Robinson, who raced all the way into the end zone to put the Dragons up 24–0.

Two minutes later, McKeever tossed a pass that was intercepted by Nathaniel Hudson. On his way to the goal, Hudson lost control of the ball, but as the bounces had gone all afternoon, the Dragons recovered at the Wildcat eight.

Three plays later, Carter skirted around the right end to cross the goal line and lift the Walker lead to 30–0.

Armstrong dodged a possible sixth strike when Walker's Leroy Cooper intercepted a Wildcat pass and returned it thirty-nine yards to the sixteen. Two plays later, the Dragons fumbled, and William Harris recovered the ball back at the twenty-nine to give the orange and blue one last chance to avoid a shutout.

After moving to the forty, Milton McCoy broke free on an eighteen-yard run to the Walker forty-two. Hurrying to get the ball in play, Clyde Cornish gained nine to the thirty-three, but the clock ran out on the Wildcats before another snap could be recorded.

While the offense had scored three of the Dragons' touchdowns, the star of the day was the defense. Led by Robinson, Cowens, Jim Epps, Bob Lanier and Ralph Williams, Walker completely dominated the Wildcats until well after the game's outcome had been decided. Allowing just 116 yards of total offense, the Dragons recorded six turnovers, four interceptions and two fumble recoveries.

Maggie Walker	6	6	6	12	**30**
Armstrong	0	0	0	0	**0**

W: Cole fifty-seven-yard pass from Tisdale (PAT failed)
W: Tisdale one-yard run (PAT failed)
W: Cowens twenty-five-yard pass interception (PAT failed)
W: Robinson forty-yard pass interception (PAT failed)
W: Carter eight-yard run (PAT failed)

Timeline Timeout

In his first Classic game as Maggie Walker's Head Coach, John "Pop" Williams's Green Dragons scored no points in a 0–0 tie with Armstrong in 1949. In his final game, played on November 29, 1959, his team rolled to a 30–0 rout. And in between, his quiet but firm leadership earned him the nickname "Pop."

Born in Norfolk, Williams started at Booker T. Washington High School and was an all-CIAA tight end at Virginia Union University, as well as a standout in the 440-yard dash for the Panthers.

Williams arrived at Maggie L. Walker High that first season in 1938 and served as assistant coach until "Stretch" Gardner stepped down after the 1948 season. Taking over in 1949, Williams led the Green Dragons to a 6-3-1 record that ended with the scoreless tie in the Classic. In 1950, Walker went 8-2-0. Then came 1951.

The Dragons were loaded with talent and showed it on the field as they outscored all the opposition 338–6, went 10-0-0, won the Classic 6–0 and were named the VIA State Champions.

Williams finished his stint as the Walker head coach with a record of 66-27-10 and was 5-3-3 in the Classic.

Halftime

It has been said that the Classic was actually a football game that interrupted a fashion show. In many ways, that interpretation holds more than just a grain of truth.

In fact, the Saturday afternoon football game wrapped up a week of festivities that started the previous Monday. All week, the schools held "loyalty days" and pep rallies and students were required to wear school colors every day.

By Saturday morning, Jackson Ward was alive with activities such as wheelbarrow races, peanut rolls and the return of long absent friends and relatives.

As game time neared, the crowds headed to City Stadium, many on foot and others in cars painted green and white or orange and blue. Richard Waller Jr. recalled that his family car was four toned, as his parents were loyal Wildcats and he and his sister were Dragons.

Once the crowds began to file into the stands, the two rival schools' marching bands began to try and outdo each other in a contest that climaxed at halftime as they were given a chance to shine. Also on show were the cadet corps and the annual naming of Miss Armstrong and Miss Walker, elected by their respective schools.

Postgame was highlighted in the early years as first the O.P. Chiles' trophy and then the Tishman Cup were awarded to the winning team. By nightfall, clubs and social halls were filled with dancing as another citywide reunion wound down.

SECTION III

Third Quarter

1960–1970

"Cannonball" Takes Over

November 26, 1960

It isn't often that Pennsylvania Avenue in Washington, D.C., and Lombardy and Leigh Street in Richmond have something in common. But in the fall of 1960, a bond was shared by both.

After a long stint as an assistant coach, Fred "Cannonball" Cooper replaced John Williams as the head man at Maggie Walker. In Washington, President-elect John F. Kennedy was preparing to move into the White House.

For the Dragons and their new mentor, the season was the strongest since the 1951 team finished 10-0-0 and won the VIA state title. The 1960 squad had much in common with that '51 edition, despite a 7-1-0 record. A high-scoring offense and stifling defense placed the Dragons in the heart of the VIA state title fight up to the final week.

Standing in the Dragons' path, Armstrong also mirrored the squad that had faced Walker back in 1951. The Wildcats entered the game with a 4-2-0 record, and Maxie Robinson was at the helm.

When November 26 arrived with warm weather, seventeen thousand spectators arrived at City Stadium as the twenty-third Classic kicked off at 2:00 p.m., almost a month after Maggie Walker's most recent contest.

That layoff was obvious as the game opened, and the Dragons didn't get on track until nearly seven minutes had passed. Possessing the ball at the Wildcat forty-nine, Berry Carter tossed a pass that Nathaniel Hudson grabbed at the fifteen and ran into the end zone. The PAT run failed, and Walker was up 6–0.

Before the quarter ended, the Dragons struck again. William Gordon broke free for a thirty-eight-yard run to the Armstrong twenty-four.

Two plays later, Walker faced third and seven at the twenty-one when Carter tossed a touchdown pass to James Cooper. Up 12–0, the Dragons went for the PAT, but a conversion pass from Melvin Swann to Hudson failed on the last play of the period.

Up 12–0 and appearing to be in control of the game, the Dragons suddenly ran out of steam.

For the remainder of the second quarter, it was the Walker defense that took over, holding the Wildcats to zero first downs and staging a dramatic goal stand.

Pinned back deep, the Dragons tried to open up with a pass that was intercepted by Aubrey Henderson, and Armstrong took over at the Walker seventeen.

The Wildcats gained nine yards to the eight, only to look down and see the ball lying one yard short of the first down marker. The Dragons took over, and the half ended with Walker up by two touchdowns.

For most of the third period, defense and punts ruled before Armstrong got a break. Henry Coles recovered a Walker fumble at the Dragon forty-two as the final period began.

Keyed by a twelve-yard pass from Stanley Brown to Milton Rose, the Wildcats put together a ten-play drive that moved the ball to the Dragon seven. After the ball was advanced to the one, Charles Saunders sneaked over from the one, and suddenly Armstrong was back in the game as the Walker lead was cut to 12–6. Robert Page kicked the PAT, and immediately Armstrong was within one touchdown of taking the lead.

But the Walker defense, led by the play of Hutson, James Chappelle, James Cooper, Stewart Miles and Irvin Miles, stood up and forced the Wildcats to burn valuable time on three straight drives that ended in punts. Doing everything they could to hold Armstrong at bay, the Dragons even resorted to several punts on third down situations.

Then, with just a minute left on the clock, the Wildcats were in possession at their own forty-five. A nineteen-yard pass from Saunders to Rose advanced the ball to the Walker thirty-four, but four consecutive incomplete passes later, the Dragons took over, ran out the clock and celebrated their second straight Classic victory. Cannonball had his first.

Third Quarter

Maggie Walker	12	0	0	0	**12**
Armstrong	0	0	0	7	**7**

W: Hutson forty-nine-yard pass from Carter (run failed)
W: Cooper twenty-one-yard pass from Carter (pass failed)
A: Saunders one-yard run (Page kick)

Maxie's "Sweetest Win"

November 25, 1961

If not for Armstrong's opening game 20–19 loss to Huntington, the 1961 Classic would have been the first time since 1942 that both the Wildcats and Green Dragons had entered the game undefeated. After that early setback, the orange and blue went on a six-game winning streak and entered the game 6-1-0. Maggie Walker entered the game even stronger, riding a fifteen-game winning streak that dated back to 1960.

Entering the game with an 8-0 record, Walker was tied with Carver of Newport News for the VIA state title. A win would set up a possible playoff with Carver.

When eighteen thousand fans packed City Stadium on a clear, chilly Saturday afternoon, everyone expected a truly "classic" Classic.

Armstrong struck first early in the opening period. On the game's first possession, the Wildcats moved to the Dragon thirty-eight on runs by Ollie Hendrick and Walter Peterson. Quarterback Chester Saunders then faked to Hendrick as four Wildcat receivers flooded the Dragon defensive backfield. Saunders connected with Peterson, who pulled in the ball on the run for a quick touchdown.

Raymond Jenkins kicked the extra point, and with the game just three minutes and forty-five seconds off the clock, the Wildcats were up 7–0.

The remainder of the period turned into a defensive battle, and early in the second quarter Walker's defense came up with the big play.

The 1961 Armstrong Wildcat football team. *1962* Armstrong Rabza.

Shortly after the teams had exchanged ends of the field, Armstrong lined up to punt the ball out from under the shadow of its own goal posts. But Warren Robertson broke through the line and blocked Saunders's kick. Albert Rosier picked up the ball at the eleven and ran over for the score to pull the Dragons to within a point at 7–6.

Robertson kicked the point after, and the game was tied 7–7. Temporarily.

After the teams had exchanged possessions, Walker quarterback Melvin Swann got off a short punt that gave the Wildcats the ball at the Dragons' twenty-nine.

On first and second down, Saunders attempted to move the ball through the air but twice threw incompletes. On his third straight pass, he connected with Henry Jones, who was able to get to the twenty, where the ball was spotted for a fourth and one.

Saunders faded back, scanned the field and saw end Thomas Hubbard open at the ten. The two connected, and Hubbard ran into the end zone standing up. Jenkins split the uprights. As the first half ended, the Wildcats were up 14–7 and had completely shut down Walker's offense, which had averaged over twenty points a game before entering the contest.

The third period continued the defensive battle that had started in the first as the lone offensive drive saw Armstrong advance to the Walker twenty-six only to be turned away.

As the game neared its end and the fans clad in orange and blue awaited their first chance to brag since 1958, the Walker offense suddenly came alive.

With just minutes left on the clock, the Dragons started one final drive at their own thirty-six. Swann gained twenty-four yards on a quarterback sneak that set the Wildcats back on their heels. He then tossed a twelve-yard pass to Marshall Corbin that placed the Dragons at the Armstrong twenty-eight.

With less than a minute left on the clock, Gilbert Carter tossed the ball toward the end zone, where it was intercepted by Jenkins. The Wildcats went wild as the final seconds ticked off and Armstrong left the field as Classic champions in what Head Coach Maxie Robinson called his "sweetest win" ever.

When the final statistics were totaled, the true nature of the role the defenses had played came to light.

Behind the efforts of Jenkins, Rudolph Tompkins and Leonard Gray, the Wildcats held the Dragons to just eighty-three yards of total offense, seventy-one coming on the ground. Walker registered four first downs, one in the first half and two on the final desperation drive.

The numbers for Armstrong were little better as defensive standouts Willie Lanier and Rozier held the Wildcats to fifty-five yards of rushing, although Saunders completed six of thirteen passes for ninety-nine yards.

Armstrong	7	7	0	0	**14**
Maggie Walker	0	7	0	0	**7**

A: Peterson thirty-eight-yard pass from Saunders (Jenkins kick)
W: Rozier eleven-yard blocked punt return (Robertson kick)
A: Hubbard twenty-yard pass from Saunders (Jenkins kick)

A State Champion (Act Three)

November 24, 1962

For one entire year, Maggie Walker had been waiting for this day. For one year, the Dragons and their fans had to carry the thought that, if not for a late interception, Walker could have vied for the VIA Group I state title and gone undefeated.

Since the third week of the 1960 season, the Dragons were 24-1 and had outscored their opponents by a total of 662 points to 99. But that one loss. That one loss was to Armstrong.

On a mission, the Green Dragons entered the game at 9-0-0, having outscored their opponents 315–18. Awaiting them were a scrappy Armstrong eleven on a five-game winning streak after dropping a season-opening loss.

Twenty thousand spectators gathered for the twenty-fifth Classic to see what would happen. They were to find out quickly.

On the game's first possession, Armstrong quarterback Leon Ward's pass to Clayton Bolling was picked off by Norman Moore at midfield. With Michael Johnson, Daryl Johnson and Robert Brooks carrying the load, Walker drove down the field to reach the Armstrong seven.

It was Michael Johnson who got the final call, going off left tackle into the end zone to give the Green Dragons a 6–0 advantage. William Scott booted the extra point, and after just one possession, Walker was up 7–0.

On the Wildcats' ensuing possession, Armstrong was forced to punt, giving the Green Dragons the ball at the Armstrong thirty-seven. Behind the rushing of both Johnsons, Walker moved the ball to the one.

Facing a fourth and goal, Gilbert Carter called a play that sent the Johnsons in motion heading in opposite directions. Carter then quickly pitched the ball to D. Johnson, who saw Moore standing alone in the end zone and flipped it to him for an easy score. Scott's kick for the extra point was off the mark, but as the period ended, Maggie Walker was up 13–0.

After all the action in the opening quarter, the second turned into a defensive struggle. The highlight was Armstrong's Henry Elam. His defensive play directly led to two Maggie Walker punts, and the half ended with the Dragons still holding a 13–0 advantage.

With the defenses controlling the game's tempo for most of the third period, Walker finally got back on track offensively.

On a first and ten at his own forty-nine, Carter connected with D. Johnson on a pass play that covered forty-one yards to the Armstrong seven. On the ensuing play, D. Johnson scored on an off-tackle run. Scott connected on the PAT, and with two minutes and fifty-eight seconds left before the game entered the final period, Walker was up 20–0.

One possession later, Walker was back on offense, with the ball at its own forty-nine early in the fourth quarter. Carter tossed a pass that

M. Johnson pulled in. Sidestepping several Armstrong defenders, he covered the fifty-one yards and crossed the goal line. The Dragons were up 26–0.

Scott was good on his third PAT kick, and with the Walker fans sensing an undefeated season, the Dragons went up 27–0.

With time running out, Armstrong avoided the shutout when, after moving the ball to the Dragon thirteen, Ward pitched the ball to Ollie Hendrick. Hendrick in turn pulled up and tossed a touchdown pass to Joseph Thorpe. Noah Barnes booted the extra point, and the score was 27–7.

On the ensuing kickoff, the Dragons fumbled, and Henry Jones recovered the ball at the Walker twenty-eight. After a thirteen-yard loss, the Wildcats called the same play that they had scored on as Ward hit Hendrick with a pass behind the line of scrimmage. Hendrick then passed to Bolling, whose diving catch moved the ball to the four with twenty-eight seconds left.

Walter Peterson got the call and ran in for the score to pull the Wildcats to 27–13. Barnes's PAT failed, and on the final kickoff, Walker retained possession. After two plays, the Dragons wrapped up the Classic, an undefeated season and the VIA State Championship.

They also started a Classic run that no one in attendance could have foreseen.

Maggie Walker	13	0	7	7	**27**
Armstrong	0	0	0	13	**13**

W: M. Johnson seven-yard run (Scott kick)
W: Moore one-yard pass from D. Johnson (kick failed)
W: D. Johnson seven-yard run (Scott kick)
W: M. Johnson fifty-one-yard pass from Carter (Scott kick)
A: Thorpe thirteen-yard pass from Hendrick (Barnes kick)
A: Peterson three-yard run (PAT failed)

TAKING ADVANTAGE OF THE LITTLE THINGS

November 30, 1963

Eight days. That was all that had passed since November 22. In Dallas eight days earlier, President John F. Kennedy had been assassinated. Across the country, football games were cancelled and sports suspended as a shocked nation tried to come to terms with what had happened. But at times such as the country was wrestling with, it is sometimes best to go on with what has helped one through the pain.

On November 30, before eighteen thousand spectators, Maggie Walker and Armstrong met for the twenty-sixth annual Classic with more than just pride on the line.

The Dragons, at 6-1-0, were still in contention for the state VIA title. The Wildcats, at 5-1-0, were heavier than Walker, and a win would secure the Virginia Interscholastic Association Central District championship.

After Walker was forced to punt on its first possession, the Dragons took advantage of a muffed reception and regained the ball at the Wildcat thirty-two.

On first down, Daryl Johnson, who finished the game with seventy-eight yards on ten carries, took the ball off right tackle and raced the entire distance for a score that left the Walker fans roaring and the Armstrong fans stunned.

Robert Chavis stepped onto the field and kicked the PAT, and with just one successful play on offense, Walker was up 7–0.

Some of the eighteen thousand fans who gathered for the 1963 Classic. *1964 Armstrong Rabza.*

The 1963 Maggie Walker Green Dragon football team. *1963* Maggie L. Walker Dragon.

On the ensuing kickoff, Woodrow Pierce misplayed the ball, giving possession right back to the Dragons.

After driving the ball to the Wildcat five, the Green Dragons turned it back over on downs. Armstrong moved the ball to the twelve, and quarterback Harold Pride faded back to his two and attempted a pass.

It was caught—by Walker's Douglas Battle. Battle returned the ball to the end zone, and the Dragons were up 13–0. Chavis kicked the extra point, and as the opening period ended, Walker was up 14–0.

For all the fireworks of the first quarter, the second produced no points and little offense, and when the half was over, the scoreboard remained unchanged.

In the final period, the Wildcats coughed up the ball, and Hamilton Perkins recovered the fumble for the Dragons. Two plays later, Michael Johnson took the ball, spotted Daryl Johnson downfield and passed the ball in his direction. Coming up on defense, Wildcat Isaiah Seal arrived at the same time as the ball.

After a struggle for control of the pigskin, Johnson came away with it, broke free at the ten and crossed the goal line. Chavis made it three for three on PATs, and the Dragons extended their advantage to 21–0.

Armstrong avoided the shutout when Ollie Hendrick scored on an eight-yard run, and William Tyler added the PAT.

While the Dragons celebrated their second straight Classic championship, the fourth in the past five years, the Wildcats could only shake their heads.

On the whole, Armstrong out-gained Walker 224 yards to 201. Woodrow Pierce had rushed for 75 yards and Ollie Hendrick, 58. But two fumbles and an intercepted pass all but handed the Dragons the win and the trophy.

Maggie Walker	14	0	0	7	**21**
Armstrong	0	0	0	7	**7**

W: D. Johnson thirty-two-yard run (Chavis kick)
W: Battle ten-yard pass interception (Chavis kick)
W: D. Johnson forty-four-yard pass from M. Johnson (Chavis kick)
A: Hendrick eight-yard run (Tyler kick)

FINALLY, A THREE-PEAT

November 28, 1964

The adage is that bad things come in threes. For Maggie Walker, the number three hovered over the 1964 Classic showdown against Armstrong. From 1960 through 1963, the Dragons had lost just three games. Already in 1964, they had lost three games and stood at 5-3-0. Now they faced the task of achieving a feat no team in the history of the Classic had reached: three straight wins.

Standing in their way was an Armstrong team that entered the game 5-1-1. When an overflow crowd of twenty-two thousand packed into City Stadium on the Saturday after Thanksgiving, the number three was standing in the shadows.

Armstrong received the opening kickoff. After moving the chains once, it came up inches short of a second first down and punted.

Maggie Walker quarterback Aldophus Maples connected with Kermit Foster on a pass that covered eight yards before Foster was nailed by Wildcat Don Ross and the ball was jarred loose.

Ross picked up the fumble and reached the Walker twenty-seven. On first down, Harold Pride tossed a pass that tight end Isaiah Seal pulled in at the eighteen and ran in for a touchdown. The extra point failed, and Armstrong was up 6–0 just three minutes and forty seconds into the game.

With neither team threatening, the score remained unchanged until the second quarter.

Facing a fourth and five at their own eighteen, the Wildcats attempted to punt, but Stanley Abrams broke free and blocked the kick, and the Dragons recovered the ball at the six.

Three plays later, Walker faced fourth and goal at the three. Maples took the snap and pitched back to Leroy Sledge at the five. Breaking a tackle, Sledge ran into the end zone and tied the game at 6–6. That score stood as the teams entered the intermission.

The third quarter belonged to the Wildcats. Reaching the Walker twenty-one, Pride connected with Maurice Pope on a touchdown pass, and Dennis Clarke's extra point kick gave Armstrong a 13–6 advantage entering the final quarter.

But then the Dragons roared back.

After failing to move the ball on third down, the Wildcats punted. The kick was pulled in on the twenty by Sledge, who broke free out to midfield. Using a key block from Robert Chavis, he outran three Wildcats and completed an eighty-yard return for a touchdown.

In one play, the game was now 13–12. Chavis missed on the PAT, but momentum had shifted to the Dragons.

On the ensuing kickoff, the Wildcats moved the ball to their own forty-seven, but a series of penalties pushed Armstrong back to its own ten and the punt to get the ball away traveled just twenty-eight yards to the thirty-eight.

Maples gained five yards on first down, and a major penalty against Armstrong moved the ball to the eighteen. But the Dragons were then dropped for a seven-yard loss back to the twenty-five.

With Maples setting up in the shotgun, he tossed Sledge a screen pass that was caught at the line of scrimmage. Breaking free, Sledge covered twenty-five yards into the end zone, and Walker grabbed an 18–13 advantage. Robert Friend kicked the extra point, and the Dragons held on for a 19–13 win.

Despite being outperformed in every statistic category, Walker used three touchdowns from Sledge to extend its advantage over Armstrong in the Classic to 13-8-5 and to win three straight for the first time ever.

Maggie Walker	0	6	0	13	**19**
Armstrong	6	0	7	0	**13**

A: Seal twenty-seven-yard pass from Pride (kick failed)
W: Sledge three-yard run (kick failed)
A: Pope twenty-one-yard pass from Pride (Clark kick)
W: Sledge eighty-yard punt return (kick failed)
W: Sledge twenty-five-yard pass from Maples (Friend kick)

A State Champion (Act Four)

November 27, 1965

For the third time since the Classic was first played in 1938, clouds of conflict darkened the horizon. In a tiny Southeast Asian nation called Vietnam, the ancient gods of war again were awakened. But for now, that was a world away, and as the showdown between Maggie Walker and Armstrong neared, the anticipation rose. By the Friday before the game, over thirteen thousand pregame tickets had been sold.

When the kickoff of the twenty-eighth Classic approached at 2:00 p.m. on November 27, the climax of a season once again arrived. For Maggie Walker, with a record of 8-1-0, a fourth straight Classic win was on the line, as well as the Central District and State Group I VIA championship.

For 5-2-0 Armstrong, the only title to play for was the Classic, one that the Wildcats had failed to obtain since 1961.

A record crowd of twenty-four thousand filled City Stadium on a warm but overcast afternoon, and the Dragons of Maggie Walker were favored to extend their winning streak over Armstrong to an unprecedented fourth straight game. What was totally unexpected was how they would do so.

Having stopped the Wildcats on the opening possession, the Dragons had taken one play to reach their own thirty-eight. The Dragons called a running play, with Leroy Sledge plowing into the middle of the line. Richard

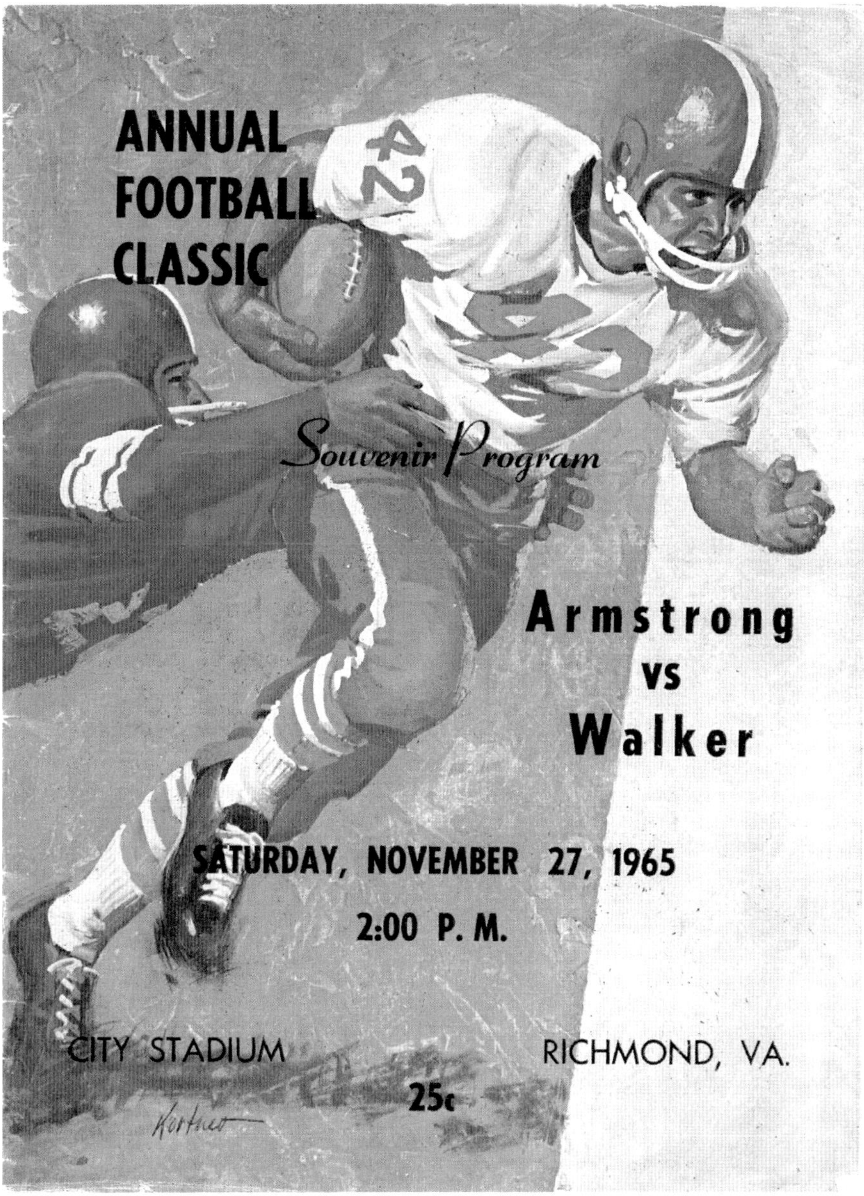

The 1965 game-day program. *Courtesy of John Dorman.*

Top: The 1965 Maggie Walker Green Dragon football team (state VIA champions). *1966* Maggie L. Walker Dragon.

Bottom: Armstrong's William James (number 36) gains yardage in the 1965 Classic. *1966* Armstrong Rabza.

Henderson and Charles Fox opened up just enough of a seam for Sledge to squeeze through, and he did the rest, rambling sixty-two yards for the game's first score.

John Winston attempted the extra point but missed, and the Dragons were up 6–0.

In the second period, Sledge got off a punt that went out of bounds at the Armstrong five. On second down, Walker linebacker Nathaniel Johnson's tackle of the Wildcat running back jarred the ball loose and back into the end zone. In the ensuing scramble, Winston, who also played defensive end, recovered the pigskin for the Dragon's second score.

But for the second time, Winston was off on the PAT kick, and the first half ended with Walker leading 12–0.

After the third period proved to be nothing more than a defensive standoff, the game entered the final quarter with Walker up by twelve.

As the clock began to wind down and the Walker fans anticipated the win, the Dragons faced fourth down at their own twenty-three. Sledge, whose punts had robbed the Wildcats of decent field position all game, got off a sixty-seven-yard boomer that died at the Armstrong twenty.

On second down, Wildcat quarterback Ronnie Hurt fumbled the ball, and Winston recorded his second fumble recovery of the game.

As the game entered its final moments, the Dragons faced fourth down at the twenty. On the final play of the game, Nathaniel Washington lofted a pass to Carlton Yates. Yates grabbed the pass, reached the end zone and, as the Walker fans stormed the field, heaved the ball into the stands as the clock read "0:00."

In winning the twenty-eighth Classic, Walker extended its lead in the series to fourteen wins, nine losses and five ties. Leroy Sledge was the difference for the Dragons, but not for the reason that would have been expected. While Sledge did lead all rushers with 104 yards, 62 came on one carry.

What Sledge did to change the game was not with his feet but with his foot. It was his punting that pinned the Wildcats down the whole game. When the final VIA rankings came out, the Dragons were crowned the state champions.

Maggie Walker	6	6	0	6	**18**
Armstrong	0	0	0	0	**0**

W: Sledge sixty-two-yard run (kick failed)
W: Winston fumble recovery in end zone (kick failed)
W: Yates twenty-yard pass from Washington (no attempt)

Just Follow the Bouncing Ball

November 26, 1966

The continued draw that the Classic had become would make the twenty-ninth meeting between Maggie Walker and Armstrong the top attended event at City Stadium in 1966. The University of Richmond–William and Mary game drew five thousand. Twenty-two thousand spectators watched the Tobacco Bowl matchup between Virginia Tech and Vanderbilt, and Thomas Jefferson–John Marshall attracted just fifteen hundred.

But the Classic was the Classic. When twenty-eight thousand fans began to overfill the stands, they once again stood as the biggest crowd at a sporting event in Richmond. And nothing to play for but pride was no reason not to be there.

Coming off the state title in 1965, Maggie Walker was out of that race in 1966, with a 6-2-0 record entering the showdown. Armstrong's record was 5-2-0.

It didn't take long for the game's first big break to occur and the tone for the afternoon to be set.

The Wildcats received the opening kickoff and on first down were nailed with a penalty. The second snap was fumbled, and Walker's Calvin Davis recovered at the Wildcat eight.

On third and goal at the four, quarterback George Johnson and end Clyde Harrison connected for a touchdown pass.

Nathaniel Jeter booted the extra point with just one minute and fifty seconds off the clock. Although many fans were not yet in their seats, the Dragons were up 7–0.

When the crowd finally settled into place, the remainder of the quarter was nothing but a string of exchanged punts.

The second quarter opened, and once again the pattern set in the first period returned.

With the ball at its own forty, Wildcat quarterback Ronnie Hurt faded back to pass. Green Dragon end Sylvester Robinson broke off his block and nailed Hurt in the motion of passing. The ball popped up in the air and landed in the arms of onrushing Walker guard Calvin Langhorne. Langhorne raced untouched into the end zone, and as the green and white–clad Walker faithful roared, the orange and blue Wildcat supporters sat stunned.

Earl Christian was good on the extra point kick, and the Dragons led 14–0.

Minutes later, the tables were turned on Walker. Deep in their own end of the field, the Dragons fumbled at the seven, and linebacker David Lewis recovered the loose ball.

On first down, Hurt rolled out right and seven yards later was in the Walker end zone for the score. Marcellus Tucker kicked the extra point and in one play Armstrong pulled to with 14–7 as the half ended.

After a scoreless third period, the game appeared to be winding down.

With four minutes left on the clock, Armstrong took possession at its own twenty-five. As time ran down, the Wildcats moved down the field to the Walker twenty-one. Rushing to get a play off, Hurt faded back on first down and passed toward the end zone. The ball was caught. The problem was that it was cradled in the arms of Dragon Perry Briggs, who returned the interception back to the forty as time ran out.

For the game, almost all of the numbers favored the Wildcats. On the ground, Armstrong rolled up 113 yards, with Earl Morton gaining 74 and Charles Davis 65, compared to 40 total rushing yards for the Dragons.

Through the air, Hurt completed nine passes for eighty-two yards and Johnson just one for four yards. But that single completion was for a score.

For all the numbers, the only ones that counted were those on the scoreboard, and Walker walked off the field with its fifth straight Classic win.

Maggie Walker	7	7	0	0	**14**
Armstrong	0	7	0	0	**7**

W: Harrison four-yard pass from Johnson (Jeter kick)
W: Langhorne forty-yard pass interception (Christian kick)
A: Hurt seven-yard run (Tucker kick)

The Law of Averages Delayed

November 25, 1967

The year 1967 was one of great contradictions. On one hand, a war lasting a mere six days turned the political balance in the Middle East upside down. The conflict in Vietnam was escalating as more and more American troops were being sent to that small corner of the world. Yet in San Francisco, the "Summer of Love" had been declared.

In November, the contradiction was that despite featuring two teams with mediocre records, the thirtieth Classic was going to draw a crowd that was as large as any that had been seen to date at a sporting event in the city of Richmond.

Maggie Walker entered the game 5-3-0. The Green Dragons faced an Armstrong squad that had stumbled through a 3-3-1 campaign.

The big question was whether the Wildcats could break the five-game losing streak that dated back to 1962, or would the Dragons continue to dominate the series that they now led 15-9-5?

As kickoff neared on Saturday, November 25, the official ticket count was twenty-nine thousand. By the final whistle, an estimated thirty-one thousand had packed City Stadium to watch the game.

The game started as a contest hinging on which team took the best advantage of the other's turnovers.

Armstrong got the first break, recovering a fumbled punt at the Walker five. But on the ensuing play, Charles Davis lost control of the ball at the goal, and Perry Briggs recovered it in the end zone for a touchback.

With time running out in the opening period, Walker drove from its own thirty to the Armstrong eight with the big play coming when George Johnson and Hermann Ross connected on a forty-yard pass.

Reaching the two, Johnson went back to the air. His pass was batted into the air and fell into Wildcat Solomon Burson's arms at the seven. Ninety-three yards later, Burson crossed the Dragon goal line for the longest scoring play in Classic history, and Armstrong went up 6–0.

On the ensuing kickoff, Leroy Jones pulled in the ball at his six and was pushed out of bounds at the forty-nine after a forty-five-yard return.

Driving to the Armstrong thirty-five, the Dragons were forced to punt, but the Wildcats were flagged for roughing, and Walker got a new set of downs at the twenty.

In three plays, Walker had advanced to the nine and yet another first down. But back-to-back offside penalties push the Dragons back to the nineteen.

From there, Johnson and Briggs combined for a nineteen-yard touchdown reception that tied the score at 6–6.

As the half was running down, Armstrong drove the ball to the Walker twenty-one before Jesse Dark recovered a second Wildcat fumble and the teams went to the locker rooms tied.

The third period started with the teams alternating possession before the Dragons began a drive that started at their own twenty-seven.

Behind the running of Leroy Jones, Emmanuel Jones and Earl Morton, Walker drove seventy yards in ten plays to the Armstrong three. Morton got the call and bulled over for the score. Dark booted the extra point, and with five minutes and fifty seconds left in the period, the Dragons were up 13–6.

Earl Morton (number 35) scores the winning touchdown in the 1967 Classic. Other identifiable Green Dragons are William Gregory (number 50), Leonard Jackson (number 77), Herman Ross (number 87), Michael Walters (number 61) and Samuel Stokes (number 72). *1968* Maggie L. Walker Dragon.

Armstrong received the ensuing kickoff, and Charles Davis, who finished the game with 145 yards on the ground, gained 31 yards in three carries. He then gained an additional 19 yards on a pass from Lafayette Merchant that moved the ball to the Dragon thirty-two.

Then, on first down, the Wildcats coughed up the ball, and Dark recovered the fumble at the Walker twenty-seven.

The final period saw the Wildcats put together three drives, but each ended with Armstrong turning the ball over on downs as the Walker defense held.

In a game marked by five turnovers and 216 yards in penalties, the Dragons made fewer mistakes and claimed their sixth straight Classic.

Maggie Walker	0	6	7	0	**13**
Armstrong	6	0	0	0	**6**

A: Burson ninety-three-yard pass interception (kick failed)
W: Briggs nineteen-yard pass from Johnson (kick failed)
W: Morton three-yard run (Dark kick)

Change and Controversy

November 30, 1968

If 1967 had been a year of contradictions, 1968 was one of change and controversy. From Soviet tanks in the streets of Prague, Czechoslovakia, to black power salutes at the Mexico City Olympics, the summer of 1968 was anything but one of love. From the Tet Offensive to the Democratic Convention in Chicago, the streets were filled with violence. The assassinations of Martin Luther King Jr. and Bobby Kennedy shocked the nation.

But in Richmond, one of the biggest changes of all occurred on September 6. Before sixteen thousand spectators, Maggie Walker played the previously all-white John Marshall at City Stadium. And it was a Capital District game.

On the football field, segregation was dead.

As the VIA was shutting down with impeding desegregation, Maggie Walker and Armstrong were admitted into the Virginia High School League, and while not eligible for the title, the two played selected teams located in the city of Richmond.

Defeating John Marshall 7–6, the Dragons routed first-year John F. Kennedy 37–0. Armstrong opened with a 27–0 win over George Wythe, routed Kennedy 66–0 and shutout Jayem 26–0.

When both had finished their pre-Classic seasons, Walker stood 8-1-0 and Armstrong 6-1-2.

Then, with just two weeks left before the game, it was determined that Armstrong had used two ineligible players. The team forfeited six wins and a tie to officially stand at 0-8-1 when November 30 rolled around. However, the Wildcats were still considered a decided favorite.

As thirty thousand spectators gathered at City Stadium, the Dragons opted to go to a defense known as "Gap 8" in an attempt to keep the Wildcats from going wide with quarterback McDaniel Anderson and running back Arthur Alexander.

The opening period started with Armstrong playing the favored role when Michael Randolph picked up a Walker fumble and returned the ball to the Dragon twenty-eight.

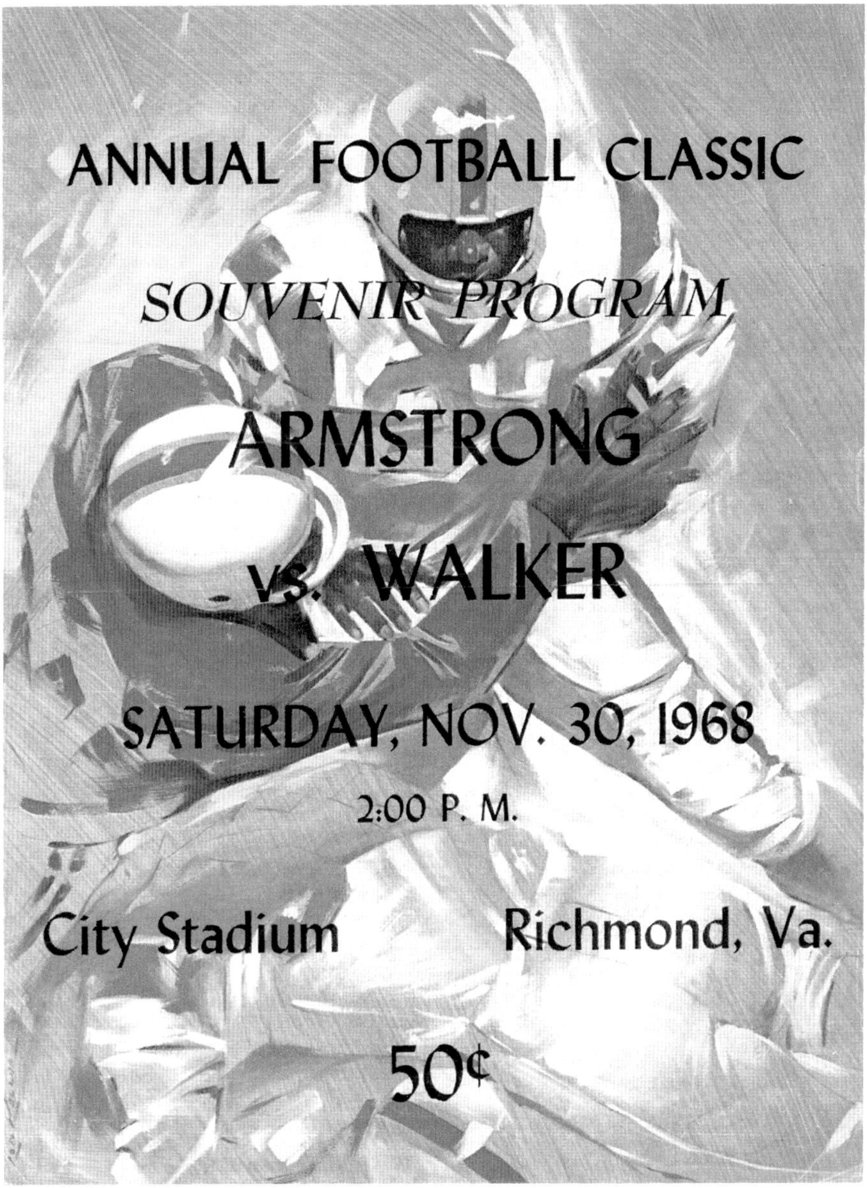

The 1968 game-day program. *Courtesy of Art Utley.*

Four plays gained just five yards as the Dragon defense knocked down two Anderson passes, and Walker took over on downs.

On third down, Walker quarterback Larry Manley was dropped for a seven-yard loss by Melvin Rose and William Ransome. The Dragons punted, and the Wildcats took over at their own thirty-one.

Using a thirty-nine-yard pass from Anderson to Archie Dabney, Armstrong drove to the Walker four before losing five yards and turning the ball over on downs back at the nine.

After two shots at the Walker goal, Armstrong came up empty. It was then Walker's time to move the ball.

A forty-six-yard pass from Manley to Hermann Ross keyed an eleven-play, ninety-yard drive as the Dragons reached the Armstrong one. With just over eight minutes left in the second quarter, Manley scored on fourth and goal, and Walker was up 6–0.

The remainder of the half settled into a defensive struggle as Walker's plan worked, and the lone highlight came when Alexander Wiggens intercepted a Wildcat pass at the Armstrong forty-eight.

The third period saw the Dragon defense start strong when Jesse Dark recovered a Wildcat fumble at the Armstrong forty-five on the second play of the half. But it wasn't until there were just over five minutes left in the quarter that either team's offense stirred, and then it was because of a miscue.

After the Dragons misplayed a punt deep in their end of the field, Byron Bogans recovered for the Wildcats at the fourteen. Three plays later, Anderson broke free of the grasp of Jonathan Tinsley and ran in for the tying touchdown. The PAT attempt failed, but the game was even at 6–6.

The Dragons regained momentum before the quarter was over when James Hardy pulled in a Wildcat punt and returned the ball to the Armstrong twenty.

The Dragons got a huge boost when the Wildcats were flagged for pass interference at the four, opening the door for Manley's scoring pass to Dark with just over eight minutes to play. Dark's PAT was blocked by William Lomax, but Walker was up 12–6.

After stopping Armstrong for zero yards on three plays, Walker regained possession on its own forty-seven. Behind the running of LaWalter Blount, the Dragons advanced to the nine.

On first down, Manley hit Murray Wood as Wood cut back at the goal posts for a touchdown, and with just barely four minutes left, Maggie Walker was up 18–6 and on the verge of its seventh straight Classic win.

As the clock ran down on the Wildcats for yet another Classic loss, Anderson tossed a thirty-five-yard pass to Jonathan Bailey, and Armstrong

Armstrong's Melvin Rose (number 52 in white) brings down a Maggie Walker running back in the 1968 Classic. Also pictured are Wildcats William Ransome (number 74), Andrew McWilliams (number 33) and Calvin Beaver (number 55). Maggie Walker's Addison Mines (number 76) comes up too late. *1969* Maggie L. Walker Dragon.

reached the Walker thirty-one. On the game's final play, Anderson was intercepted by Fred Fox in the end zone.

"Gap 8" made sure at least one thing hadn't changed: Walker won.

Maggie Walker	0	6	0	12	**18**
Armstrong	0	0	6	0	**8**

W: Manley one-yard run (kick failed)
A: Anderson ten-yard run (kick failed)
W: Dark four-yard pass from Manley (kick blocked)
W: Wood nine-yard pass from Manley (kick failed)

Timeline Timeout

Sometimes, one person can seem to do it all. Fewer times, one person can seem to do it all, all of the time. Arthur "Stretch" Gardner was such a man.

From the opening of Maggie Walker High in the fall of 1938, the Armstrong High and Virginia Union University graduate had been coach of almost every sport that the Green Dragons offered. While his longest stint was along the sidelines of the basketball court, where he stalked for thirty-one years, he also was the head man for track, baseball, tennis and even girls' basketball.

And from 1938 to 1948, he was the head coach of the football team. Starting from a group of eighth graders who didn't even have uniforms, he guided the program to the elite of the VIA state powers. Against the Wildcats, his record was 4-5-2, and he enjoyed a five-year stretch (1942–46) when Walker didn't lose to the Wildcats.

But wins and losses aside, respect and getting an education were what Coach Gardner passed on to his players. For all he had done, his retirement was celebrated at the halftime of the 1969 Classic.

IT WAS OVER BEFORE IT BEGAN

November 29, 1969

The 1969 Classic was one of two firsts. First, for the first year ever, both Maggie Walker and Armstrong would play full Capital District schedules and become eligible for the district title. Second, for the first time ever, Maxie Robinson was not walking the sidelines as Armstrong's head coach. Having retired in June, he was replaced by Angier Lawrence, who came over when Virginia Randolph High School in Henrico was closed.

A season that started with—or almost didn't start due to—a record James River flood by Hurricane Camille was about to end with the thirty-second Classic meeting between a 6-3-0 Maggie Walker and an Armstrong team that stood at 3-4-1.

Arthur "Stretch" Gardner is honored at his retirement during the halftime of the 1969 Classic. *From left to right*: George Jefferson; Perry Briggs, hero of the 1945 Classic; Coach Gardner; and Principal Sidney Parker. *1970* Maggie L. Walker Dragon.

By the time the thirty-second Classic kicked off, twenty-eight thousand spectators were packed in the stands, but an estimated six thousand additional fans were still walking in, greeting, hugging and back-slapping old friends. By the time that extra fan base had found seats, or rather places to stand, the crowd had swelled to thirty-four thousand. And the score was already 13–0, Walker.

On the opening kickoff, Dragon Ernest Walker received and promptly bobbled the ball. Regaining possession, he turned his back to the onrushing Wildcats and flipped the ball to Murray Wood. Wood took the ball and broke free for a seventy-two-yard return that put Walker up 6–0 with just twelve seconds gone off the stadium clock.

On the ensuing Armstrong possession, Reginald Ashby recovered a fumble at the Wildcat five. Facing a third and goal at the one, quarterback Andrew Miles called his own number and bulled over for the score. The PAT was good, and with three minutes off the clock, the Dragons were up 13–0.

With the period winding down, Armstrong went to the air only to have Weldon Edwards intercept a pass at the Wildcat forty. Racing the clock, Walker drove to the Wildcat five, where Derick Hilton scored on the last play of the quarter.

In the second period, Armstrong quarterback Curtis McBride broke free for a thirty-seven-yard run. After lineman Melvin Rose gained four yards on a trick play, Raymond Bowser intercepted for Walker at his own eight.

Sticking to the ground game for all but one play, the Dragons drove eighty-nine yards to the Wildcat three. From there, LaWalter Blount scored, and the first half ended with the Dragons up 25–0.

Maggie Walker's Robert Jones (in white on the ground) gains yards in the 1969 Classic. Others for Walker are Addison Mines (number 76) and Jonathan Tinsley (number 83). Wildcat defenders include George Brooks (number 72), James McBride (number 24), Ronard Betts (number 20) and Frank Morton (number 14). *1970* Maggie L. Walker Dragon.

Just as in the first half, the second barely got the crowds back into their seats before the Dragons struck one final time.

Anthony Jones pulled in an interception and returned the ball back to the Armstrong twenty. After the Wildcat defense stiffened, the Dragons lost twelve yards in two plays back to the thirty-two.

Facing a third and thirty-two, Andrew Miles faded back after taking the snap and tossed a pass in the direction of Bowser. Defensive back Carl Smith came up for an attempted interception but missed as Bowser pulled in the ball at the fifteen and ran in for the score.

Up 31–0, the Dragons held on and claimed their eighth straight Classic Title.

Maggie Walker	19	6	6	0	**31**
Armstrong	0	0	0	0	**0**

W: Woods seventy-two-yard kickoff return (kick failed)
W: Miles one-yard run (Dean kick)
W: Hinton two-yard run (kick failed)
W: Blount three-yard run (kick failed)
W: Bowser thirty-two-yard pass from Miles (run failed)

It Doesn't Matter How

November 28, 1970

The road to the thirty-third Armstrong–Maggie Walker Classic began with a major bump back in August before the school year began. On August 17, federally mandated desegregation orders that included busing and redistricting were put in effect by an order from U.S. District Court judge Robert Merhige Jr. They changed the face of the City of Richmond's public school system forever.

Threats of boycotts on the opening day of school on August 31, however, never materialized, as Virginia's first Republican governor since

Action from the 1970 Classic. Maggie Walker's Maurice Henderson (number 55), Anthony George (number 63) and William Thornton (number 22) stop an Armstrong drive. *1971 Maggie L. Walker Dragon.*

Reconstruction, Linwood Holton, walked his daughter to J.F. Kennedy, the school she was assigned to under the new orders.

But the changes broke up teams and coaching staffs among the schools that made up the Capital District. When November 28 rolled around for the Classic, Maggie Walker was a mere 4-3-1. Coach Cooper had lost three key assistant coaches in redistricting, and that necessitated weaving new faces into the program.

At Armstrong, it was worse as the Wildcats struggled to a 1-7-0 record. But the biggest change was that, for the first time ever, there were five white players in the Classic. Desegregation had arrived.

With much that the Classic rested on now gone, pride was still left. As a crowd of twenty-two thousand gathered on a warm November 28, the Armstrong–Maggie Walker game entered a new and final stage.

The opening period was all Armstrong.

Starting a drive at their own forty-nine, the Wildcats took just three plays to reach the Maggie Walker one. Pushed back to the two, the Wildcats scored as James Briggs bulled over into the end zone, and for the first time since 1967, they enjoyed an edge over the Dragons.

Before the quarter was over, the Wildcats struck again.

Taking over at their own eighteen on their next possession, the Wildcats ground out twelve plays that advanced the ball fifty yards to the Walker thirty-two.

Top: The 1970 Maggie Walker football team. *1971* Maggie L. Walker Dragon.

Bottom: The 1970 Maggie Walker coaching staff. *From left to right*: Fred Cooper, Pierce Callaham, Samuel Scott, Arthur Cauthorne, Terrence O'Toole, Howard Hopkins and George Bowser. *1971* Maggie L. Walker Dragon.

Armstrong quarterback George Stanley faded back and connected with John Oliver, who didn't stop until he crossed the goal line to the delight of the long-suffering fans of the orange and blue.

The run for the two-point conversion failed, but the Wildcats were up 12–0 and had completely dominated play on the field.

But for all the fireworks in the opening quarter, the second saw the defenses settled down, and the score remained unchanged as the teams headed to the locker rooms.

Maggie Walker defenders William Thornton (number 22), Norman Randolph (number 82) and Curtis Reid (number 81) bring down an Armstrong running back in the 1970 Classic. *1971* Armstrong Rabza.

The third period was a continuation of the second as neither team produced any offense. But the fourth was a different story.

In possession at midfield and down by two touchdowns, Dragon quarterback Andrew Miles tossed passes of twenty-two yards to Anthony Leonard and twenty-four yards to Anthony Jones, and in three plays, Walker was at the Armstrong one. Robert Briggs bulled over from there, and suddenly the Dragons had pulled to 12–6

Moments later, the green and white owned the ball again, driving to the Armstrong thirty. Facing a fourth and one, Wayne Taylor took the handoff and reached the twenty-eight for a first down. Driving to the two, the Dragons tied the game 12–12 on a pass from Miles to Norman Randall with less than five minutes left.

Abandoning the running game, a desperate Armstrong went to the air. But Stanley's pass to Lewis Robinson was intercepted by William Thornton, who returned the ball back twenty-six yards to the Wildcat thirty-two.

With the clock running out, Walker drove to the seventeen, and on second down, Miles connected with Leonard, who turned downfield. At the five, Jones threw a key block, and with just a minute and fifty-five seconds left on the clock, Leonard crossed the goal line, and the Dragons completed their amazing rally to go up 18–12.

Even the bands got into the action. *1971* Maggie L. Walker Dragon.

And two minutes later, "the Streak" reached nine as the Dragons used passes, runs and a turnover to dominate just one quarter of the game, but still do enough to retain bragging rights for one more year.

Maggie Walker	0	0	0	18	**18**
Armstrong	12	0	0	0	**12**

A: J. Briggs one-yard run (kick failed)
A: Oliver thirty-two-yard pass from Stanley (run failed)
W: R. Briggs one-yard run (kick failed)
W: Randall two-yard pass from Miles (pass failed)
W: Leonard seventeen-yard pass from Miles (pass failed)

SECTION IV

Fourth Quarter

(1971–1978)

"Next Year" Finally Arrives

November 27, 1971

The 1971 Armstrong-Walker Classic was rocked to its foundation months before the game was even played. First, in June, Coach Fred "Cannonball" Cooper announced his retirement as head football coach at Maggie Walker. Having served on the Green Dragon staff for twenty-four years, his record as the Dragons' mentor from 1960 was 91-18-1 and included a 10-1 record in the Classic.

Second, in September, the Capital District ruled that both Armstrong and Maggie Walker were ineligible for the district championship. (The Classic was played after the November 12 cutoff date for eligibility to play in the newly established statewide playoffs.)

But both schools were firm. Eligible or not, the Classic stayed put on the last Saturday in November. When November 27 rolled around, the question of post eligibility remained a moot point as both teams had been eliminated from the district title earlier in the season.

Armstrong started the season slow and entered the contest 4-5-0. Maggie Walker, under new head coach Lou Anderson, who had starred for the Dragons in 1955, was 4-4-0.

When the crowd gathered at City Stadium (it had rained earlier in the day, skies were overcast and temperatures hovered at forty degrees), it numbered twelve thousand, the smallest since 1959.

The 1971 game-day program. *Courtesy of Art Utley.*

The field, left muddy from the rain, proved a hindrance for both offenses and an advantage for the defenses.

With both squads sticking primarily to a ground game, neither threatened until Walker began a ten-play, fifty-yard drive that reached the Wildcat twenty. Facing fourth and eight, quarterback Steve Turpin tossed a pass to

The 1971 Armstrong football team. *1972* Armstrong Rabza.

Anthony Leonard that came up two yards short at the fourteen, and the Wildcats took over on downs.

With the game still scoreless in the second quarter, the Dragons reached Armstrong's thirty-two. On third and six, Turpin tossed a pass toward the end zone that Wildcat Vincent Dean intercepted over the shoulder at the one, and he fell into the end zone for a touchback.

For the remainder of the period, both teams slipped and sputtered in the mud as the half ended scoreless.

The third period started as the teams exchanged punts that found the Wildcats in possession of the ball on their own twenty-six. After Marcus Harris gained six yards to the thirty-two, quarterback George Stanley called his own number in the huddle.

Getting past the line of scrimmage, Stanley cut to the sideline and wasn't caught until he covered fifty-four yards to the Walker fourteen.

Facing fourth and six at the ten, Stanley rolled to the left and tossed the ball toward the end zone. After bouncing off several players, the ball fell into the arms of James Briggs. Briggs had already fallen to the ground during the play and was lying in the end zone when he cradled the touchdown pass.

Stanley's conversion pass failed, but with just under three minutes remaining in the period, the Wildcats were up 6–0.

Armstrong's Gary Watkins heads up field with a pass from George Stanley in the 1971 Classic. *1972* Armstrong Rabza.

As the final period began, the question was whether Armstrong would hold on or Maggie Walker would come up with one more way to walk off the field Classic champs.

With five minutes and twenty-five seconds left, Armstrong took over possession at its own forty-nine, needing nothing more than to run out the clock. What it got was a twelve-play drive that finally died at the Walker nine with just a minute and twelve seconds left. The Wildcat faithful looked at one another and asked, "Is this it?"

On its last chance, Walker got as far as the Wildcat forty-five before the clock ran out. The Armstrong faithful ran out on the field and "the Streak" was no more. For the Wildcats, "next year" had finally arrived.

Armstrong	0	0	6	0	**6**
Maggie Walker	0	0	0	0	**0**

A: Briggs ten-yard pass from Stanley (pass failed)

Fred "Cannonball" Cooper (right) is congratulated on his retirement by Maggie L. Walker principal Sidney Parker at the 1971 Classic. *1972* Maggie L. Walker Dragon.

Maggie Walker's Tery Black (number 55) watches as a play in the 1971 Classic ends. *1972* Armstrong Rabza.

Timeline Timeout

The last time Armstrong had defeated Maggie Walker, in 1961, Angier Lawrence had coached Virginia Randolph High in Henrico County to a 7-1-0 record. Ten years later, Lawrence stood on the sidelines at City Stadium in his third year as the Wildcats' head coach, still seeking his first win over Maggie Walker. His first two years at Armstrong had been a far cry from the success he had enjoyed out on Mountain Road as the Typhoons' mentor. The Durham, North Carolina native came to Henrico County's VIA representative in 1953, with an undergraduate degree from North Carolina College and master's in heath education from New York University.

At Virginia Randolph, he coached football, basketball, track, golf and baseball. But when the Henrico School System fully integrated in 1969, the Typhoon players were scattered among the traditional white high schools as Randolph ceased to exist as a high school. In Richmond, Maxie Robinson retired from Armstrong after thirty-seven years, and Lawrence took the job at the Church Hill school.

In his first two seasons at Armstrong, Lawrence went 3-5-1 and 1-8-0, falling to Walker 31–0 and 18–12 in the Classic. But the 1971 Wildcats entered the game with four wins and left with five, ending a nine-game drought against the Dragons.

But more than Armstrong finally defeating Walker had changed in the long history of the Classic. Much more.

Inset picture: Angier Lawrence, Armstrong head coach, 1969–78. *1979* Armstrong Rabza.

Payback for All Those Years

November 26, 1972

For the first time since 1962, Armstrong entered the Classic as the defending champion, and Maggie Walker had spent twelve months waiting for "next year." But this year had been rough on both teams, and the Classic title was all either had to play for.

Starting the season 1-5-0, Armstrong won two straight games to enter Classic weekend 3-5-0. For Maggie Walker, the season had been the worst since 1939, and as the showdown neared, the Dragons were 2-6-0, riding a four-game losing streak.

When November 26 arrived, the *Richmond Times-Dispatch*'s front page ran a story concerning a highjacked jet in Germany, opening talks for peace in Vietnam and, most important to Richmond, a forecast for rain and temperatures in the forties. That didn't bode well for much offense between two teams that relied on their defenses.

Armstrong had won its last two games by a total of 53–6 and appeared to have finally mastered the wishbone formation. Before the crowd of ten thousand cold and damp spectators, the Wildcats, behind a forty-seven-yard run by sophomore Nathan Munford, drove the ball sixty-five yards to the Walker three. From there, Munford bulled over for the touchdown, and Armstrong led 6–0.

With neither team dealing well with the less-than-optimal field conditions, it was Armstrong's grinding running game that began to show its superiority.

Taking over at their own nineteen early in the second quarter, the Wildcats ran eight plays to the Dragon one. Quarterback Thomas McLendon called his own number and sneaked over for the score. Glenn Mason kicked the PAT to give Armstrong a 13–0 advantage, which it took into the intermission.

As the rain began to pour during the half, it was the Armstrong offensive line that took over. On their first possession of the third quarter, the Wildcats, behind the blocking of Charles Hurdle, John Taylor, Joe Harris, Anthony Bailey and Milton Bailey, reached the Walker thirteen.

Sophomore running back Ricky Crawford took the handoff and broke free for the scoring run. Mason connected on his second extra-point kick, and the Wildcats were up 20–0.

Before the period was over, the Wildcats were on the move again when Crawford lost his handle on the ball at the Walker one and fumbled into the end zone. But Milton Bailey was there and fell on the loose pigskin for the touchdown. Armstrong went up 26–0 entering the final twelve minutes.

With the defense—behind the play of Hurdle, Taylor, James Brown, Ronald Dillard, Fred Jones, Milton Smith and Anthony Bailey—thwarting the Dragon running game at every turn and keeping quarterback Steve Turpin under control, the Wildcat offense got on the scoreboard one last time.

With seven minutes and twenty-five seconds left on the clock, Armstrong was in possession at the Walker two. Lonnie McCoy got the call and bulled over for the score. Kenny Yarbrough pulled in Ervin McBride's two-point conversion pass, and the Wildcats were up 34–0.

When the official's gun ended the contest, Armstrong walked off the field with its largest margin of victory in Classic history.

Armstrong	6	7	13	8	**34**
Maggie Walker	0	0	0	0	**0**

A: Munford three-yard run (kick failed)
A: McLendon one-yard run (Mason kick)
A: Crawford thirteen-yard run (Mason kick)
A: Bailey fumble recovered in end zone (kick failed)
A: McCoy two-yard run (Yarbrough pass from McBride)

ONE HALF IS BETTER THAN NONE

November 24, 1973

War, peace and oil filled the front page of the *Richmond Times-Dispatch* on a warm November 24, 1973. For the second time in seven years, the Middle East had exploded into war. By the Saturday after Thanksgiving, peace feelers were being sent out, but talks were slow.

Timeline Timeout

With less than two months left before the 1973 Armstrong-Walker Classic, another classic was lost. On October 12, the city of Richmond was shocked and saddened when it learned that Maxie C. Robinson, head coach at Armstrong for thirty-four years, had died.

Robinson, a graduate of Armstrong, was an all-CIAA halfback at Virginia Union before restarting the Wildcats' (then called the Generals) program as a volunteer coach in 1933. In 1934, he was hired as a history teacher, and in 1938, he was also named head basketball coach.

Under his leadership, Armstrong won the state VIA football championship in 1947. But it was on the sideline of the basketball court where he shone. The Wildcats were state champions in 1941, 1945, 1959 and 1964. Known for his firmness and fairness (he once cut his own son, future news broadcasting pioneer Max Robinson, from the basketball team), his 1941 and 1964 teams were runners-up at the National Negro High School Tournaments.

He also coached track for ten years and baseball for five.

Robinson stepped down as head football coach after the 1968 season, with an 8-17-5 record in the Classic, and retired from Armstrong in 1972.

As talking was beginning to replace shooting on the battlefield, a new weapon appeared: an oil embargo. Arab countries, kingdoms and sheikdoms planned to lower or cut off oil supplies to the West if the Yom Kippur War wasn't settled soon. But in Richmond, it was Classic weekend, and at least for an afternoon, the battle would be on a football field.

After losing the opening two games of the season, Armstrong entered the Classic with a 5-2-1 record. The Green Dragons' road to the game was just the opposite, as Walker started 2-1-1 but carried a five-game losing streak to finish at 2-6-1.

The best playing conditions in several years attracted the most fans since 1970—eighteen thousand—to City Stadium. And for one half, they watched nothing; no breaking plays, no defensive stands and no points. Then the third quarter began, and a Wildcat offense that was pinned down for two quarters began to stir.

Just over four minutes into the third period, Armstrong had the ball at its own twenty-six. One play later it was up 6–0.

Maggie Walker's Eugene Lucas (number 2) is closed in on by Armstrong defenders during the 1973 Classic. *1973* Maggie L. Walker Dragon.

Nathan Munford, who was held to a net of zero yards in the first two periods, broke free and raced untouched down the sideline for the score. Ricky Crawford ran in the two-point conversion, and the Wildcats led 8–0.

On the very next series, Walker came to life behind the passing of Eugene Lucas. With the ball at the Armstrong forty-one, Lucas connected with Steve Turpin on a long scoring pass that appeared to close the score to 8–6. But back at the line of scrimmage, a yellow flag lay on the ground, and the Dragons were called for illegal procedure, nullifying the score and any hope for a Walker upset.

Leading 8–0 early in the final quarter, the Wildcats reached the Dragon nineteen. Munford took the ball around the left side for a touchdown that put Armstrong up 14–0.

On the ensuing kickoff, the Wildcats got possession back when Bernard Napier separated the Walker return man from the ball, and Lamont Kizzie recovered for Armstrong at the Green Dragon twenty-three. After three plays moved the ball to the twelve, Kermit Blount tossed a touchdown pass to Richard Fuller, and the scoreboard showed the Wildcats up 20–0.

The final Armstrong score was provided by the defense. Behind the play of James Brown, Gregory Campbell, Wilson Shannon, Robert Terry and Curtis Coles, the Wildcats held the Dragons to a minus 104 yards rushing. With Walker on its own twenty, quarterback Lucas was chased backward and tackled in the end zone by Carlton Jones for a safety and the final 22–0 margin.

Three straight years, three straight shutouts, and Armstrong had finally three-peated.

Armstrong	0	0	8	14	**22**
Maggie Walker	0	0	0	0	**0**

A: Mumford seventy-four-yard run (Crawford run)
A: Mumford nineteen-yard run (PAT failed)
A: Fuller twelve-yard pass from Blount (PAT failed)
A: Safety

The Best Game Ever?

November 30, 1974

Things in America were changing. For the first time since 1968, the country had a new president. But this chief executive didn't receive a single vote. Vice President Gerald Ford stepped into the Oval Office when President Richard Nixon resigned under the shadow of the Watergate scandal.

Things in Richmond were also changing. For the first time since 1966, Classic Saturday arrived with Maggie Walker and Armstrong entering their annual competition boasting winning records.

After back-to-back seasons that saw Walker win a total of just four games, the Green Dragons were 6-1-1 and a perfect 5-0-0 in the Capital District. While ineligible for the title, a win over Armstrong would give Walker an unblemished record against the other city schools and its first Classic win since 1970.

For the Wildcats, the most important bragging rights were those that came with winning the Classic. After winning four and losing three games leading up to the Classic, Armstrong found itself the underdog for the first time in three years.

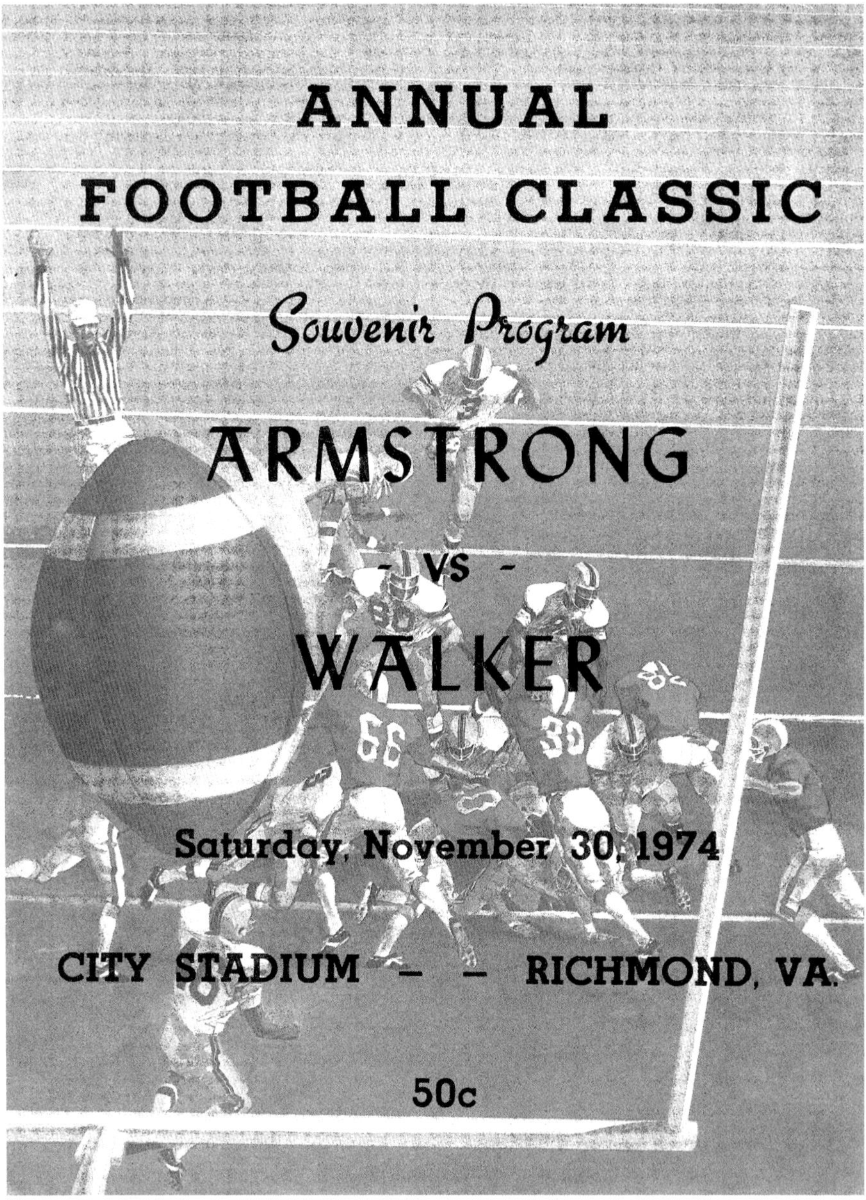

The 1974 game-day program. *Courtesy of Art Utley.*

The 1974 Armstrong Wildcat football team. *Courtesy of Art Utley.*

As twenty-one thousand spectators gathered in City Stadium on a cool, overcast afternoon for the thirty-seventh meeting between the rivals, few knew that they were about to witness what was probably the best meeting ever.

In the opening period, the Wildcats faced a first and ten at their own one-yard line. With Nathan Munford carrying the ball seven times, Armstrong drove to the Walker three. Munford then took an eighth handoff that crossed the goal line, and Armstrong was up 6–0. Munford got the call on the two-conversion run and took the ball into the end zone. The Wildcats were up 8–0.

On the ensuing kickoff, however, Everett Leonard received the ball at his eighteen and broke free for a thirty-seven-yard return to the Armstrong forty-five.

Aided by a facemask penalty called on the Wildcats, the Dragons were quickly in possession at the nine. Quarterback Eugene Lucas called his own number and bootlegged toward the goal. Just as he crossed the goal line near the flag, he was hit by two defenders and landed on the asphalt track that encircled the playing field, injuring his throwing hand.

Trailing 8–6, the Dragons rushed John Goode in from the sidelines to run the conversion play, but his keeper came up short.

Regaining possession before the quarter was over, Walker's passing attack was limited to Lucas sticking to screen passes and short attempts. His one try at a deep pattern was a disaster, as Wildcat Michael Hawkins intercepted the ball at his forty-five and returned it to the Walker thirty-five.

Running the wishbone *T* formation to near perfection, Armstrong ground out nine plays to the two. Quarterback Kermit Blount carried the ball on the tenth snap for the last two yards on a sneak to put the Wildcats up 14–6. Ricky Crawford rushed for the two-point conversion to give Armstrong a 16–6 advantage in the second period.

Then, as the opening half neared its end, with the Wildcats in possession near midfield, Blount lost control of the ball. It was recovered by Walker's Gregory Conner. Racing the clock, the Dragons went to the air as Lucas tossed ten-yard passes to running backs Bernard Eberhardt and Jeffrey Washington. The ball was advanced to the Armstrong twelve, where Lucas tossed a scoring pass to Genie Farmer. Washington added the two-point conversion run to pull Walker to 16–14 as the first half ended.

Armstrong struck quickly as the game resumed in the third quarter when Crawford broke free on a thirty-yard touchdown run. Blount added the two-point conversion, and the Wildcats were back up by ten, 24–14.

Walker recovered, drove down the field and reached the Armstrong ten moments later.

Taking the handoff from Lucas, Eberhardt pulled up and tossed a scoring pass to John Goode. Eberhardt then pulled in the two-point conversion pass from Lucas, and for the third time, the Green Dragons pulled to within two points, 24–22.

With time running out in the third period, Walker was on the move again. Washington reeled off a twenty-yard run and then lined up for an apparent punt. Lucas took the snap and flipped a five-yard pass to Clifton Wyche for the first down.

Hoping to find the Wildcats on their heels, Lucas went for pay dirt. But his pass was overthrown, and Armstrong cornerback William Thrower made a diving interception in the end zone.

For most of the final quarter, the Wildcat defense bottled up the Dragons. But with the stadium game clock running down and Walker on its own nineteen, the Dragons struck. Lucas tossed a screen pass to Eberhardt, who broke three tackles and headed up field. He was finally tackled by Bernard Napier at the Armstrong twenty-nine.

Eberhardt then ripped off a twenty-yard run off right tackle, giving the Dragons a first and goal at the Armstrong nine.

Armstrong's Nathan Munford (number 30) runs interference for Ricky Crawford as Maggie Walker's John Pegram (number 82) tries to break up a play in the 1974 Classic. *1975* Armstrong Rabza.

Action in the 1974 Classic was so hard fought that the only identifiable player is Maggie Walker's John Pegram (number 82). *1977* Armstrong Rabza.

Maggie Walker's Eugene Lucas (number 2) tries to break away from Armstrong's Michael Hawkins (number 80) in the 1974 Classic. *1975* Maggie L. Walker Dragon.

As time became a more stressful factor, Lucas attempted to hit Farmer on a corner pattern, but for the second straight play, Napier recorded a key defensive play and knocked the pass down. Lucas then tried a screen pass, only to have Dennis Winston break up the play.

With the clock reading two minutes, the Dragons opted to attempt a game-winning field goal and got two chances.

Bryant Watkins blocked Aubrey Waddy's first kick from the twenty-seven, but the Wildcats were flagged for being offside.

With everyone in the crowd standing to watch, and both sidelines straining to get a view, the second kick, now from the twenty-two, got past the line of scrimmage. But as it sailed to the goal posts, the ball went wide, and the scoreboard remained unchanged.

Two minutes later, the clock ran out on the Green Dragons, and the Wildcats walked off the field with a 24–22 Classic win.

Armstrong	8	8	8	0	**24**
Maggie Walker	6	8	8	0	**22**

A: Munford three-yard run (Munford run)
W: Lucas nine-yard run (run failed)
A: Blount two-yard run (Crawford run)
W: Farmer twelve-yard pass from Lucas (Washington run)
A: Crawford thirty-yard run (Blount run)
W: Goode ten-yard pass from Eberhardt (Eberhardt pass from Lucas)

10 and 0 and No Place to Go

November 29, 1975

Four years. For four years, Maggie Walker had left the field at City Stadium on the short end of the score against rival Armstrong.

Twelve years. It had been twelve years since a Maggie Walker team had finished unbeaten.

When November 29, 1975, arrived, the Green Dragons were on the verge of ending both streaks. Walker rolled to a 9-0-0 record and outscored its foes by an average of twenty-four to four.

But standing in the Dragons' way was an Armstrong squad that had won six and lost three. As twenty-four thousand spectators gathered at City Stadium under ideal weather conditions, the question was whether Walker could roll over all six teams in a district where it was ineligible, be the only 10-0-0 team in the state not to go to the playoffs and break a four-year losing streak in the Classic. Or was Armstrong up for a second straight upset?

One thing both teams had to deal with was the new artificial turf surface at City Stadium. From the start, Walker loved it.

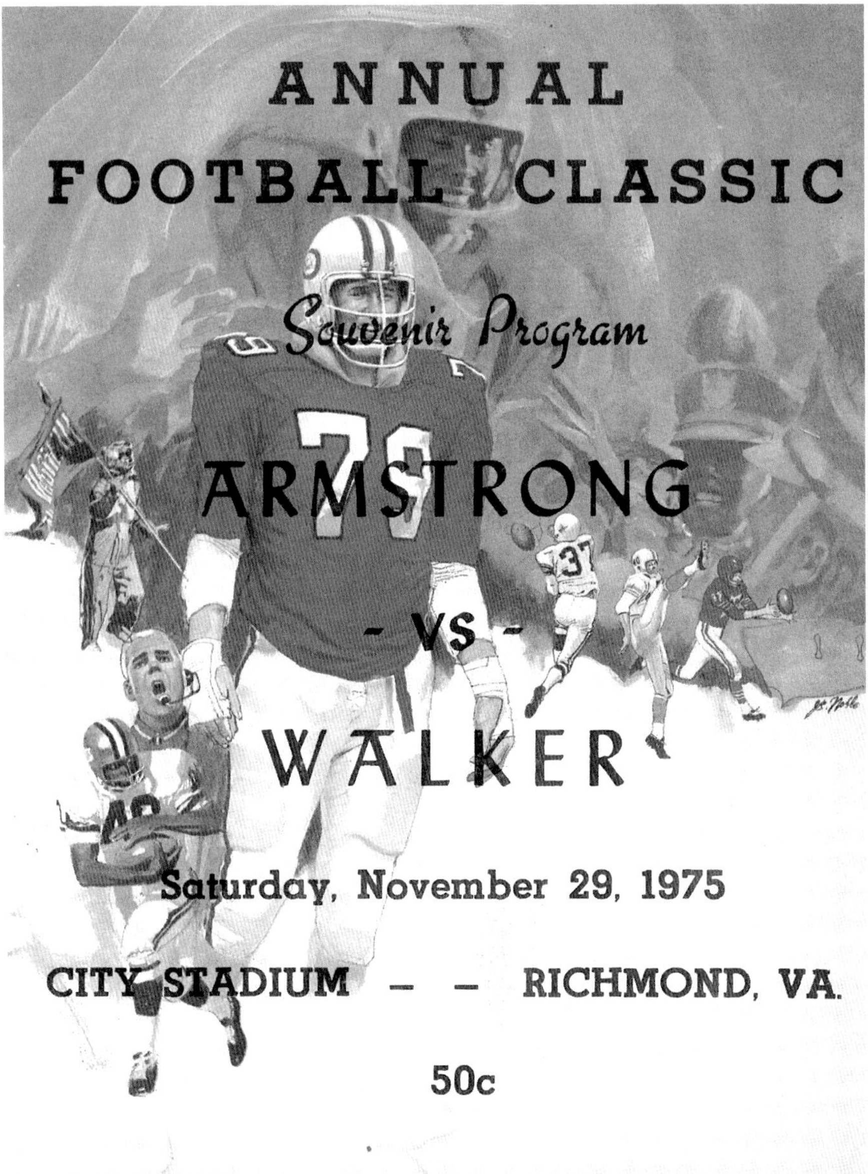

The 1975 game-day program. *Courtesy of Art Utley.*

Some of the twenty-four thousand spectators who gathered for the 1975 Classic. *1976 Armstrong Rabza.*

On their first possession, the Green Dragons, aided by a major facemasking penalty, moved the ball from their thirty-three to the Armstrong thirty-eight. Quarterback Eugene Lucas faded back to pass and hit flanker Richard Thomas at the fifteen. After bobbling the ball, Thomas gained control and raced in for the score. The attempted extra failed, but Walker was up 6–0.

On their next possession, the Dragons started at their thirty. Having switched directions when the quarters changed, Walker moved the ball to Wildcat five. Lucas called his own number, fading back and then running forward on a quarterback draw. As he crossed the goal line, the ball came loose, and Armstrong recovered in the end zone. The officials conferred, and it was determined that Lucas was in possession when he broke the plane. The touchdown stood. Eddie Lewis connected on the PAT kick, and Walker was up 13–0.

After Jeffery Washington scored on a twenty-two-yard run and Lewis's second PAT put Walker up 20–0 in the second period, the Armstrong offense came to life.

With Maurice Shands carrying much of the load, the Wildcats drove to the Dragon fifteen as the opening half was winding down. Pushed back to the twenty-seven after an ineligible receiver downfield penalty, quarterback Kermit Blount hit Thomas Wright on a pass to the ten. Trying to gain

Flanked by Jeffery Washington (number 22) and Eugene Lucas (number 2), Maggie Walker head coach Lou Anderson enjoys the 1975 Classic win over Armstrong. *1978* Maggie L. Walker Dragon.

additional yardage, Wright was hit at the five, and the ball came loose. Green Dragon defender John Pegram came through and recovered the fumble at the one, and Walker entered the half up 20–0.

In the third quarter, Washington, who rushed for 219 yards on twenty-one carries, broke free for a 41-yard touchdown run. Lewis connected on his third extra point kick, and as the game entered the final quarter, the Dragon fans were rocking in the stands, up 27–0.

This Classic just wasn't Armstrong's. The Wildcats misplayed a punt reception at their own five, and Pegram recovered his second fumble of the game. Moments later, Lucas carried the ball to the goal line from the two but fumbled into the end zone. This time the ball was live, and Arthur Cook picked the ball up for the Dragons for a 33–0 advantage.

Armstrong avoided the shutout when, with just fifty-one seconds on the clock, Blount and Shands connected on a fifty-one-yard pass-run play that crossed the goal line.

Coach Anderson had to be the happiest man on the field. Four years had just been erased in one afternoon.

Fourth Quarter

Maggie Walker	6	14	7	6	**33**
Armstrong	0	0	0	6	**6**

W: Thomas thirty-eight-yard pass from Lucas (run failed)
W: Lucas five-yard run (Lewis kick)
W: Washington twenty-two-yard run (Lewis kick)
W: Washington forty-one-yard run (Lewis kick)
W: Cook fumble recovered in end zone (kick failed)
A: Shands fifty-yard pass from Blount (run failed)

An Upset Taken Away

November 27, 1976

When asked about a big rivalry game, coaches are notorious for answering, "You can throw away the record book when we meet them." Maggie Walker coach Lou Anderson was dearly hoping that that Thanksgiving Day prayer was being said at the home of every Dragon fan everywhere.

Coming off a 10-0-0 1975 season, Anderson entered 1976 with a team missing nine starters on offense and seven on defense, and the result shouldn't have been a surprise. Still, it was a disappointment; they were 1-7-1 after nine games.

Over at Armstrong, the Wildcats were 5-3-0, and though ineligible for the title, they would finish with the same Capital District record (5-1-0) as official champion Thomas Jefferson.

When fifteen thousand spectators gathered at City Stadium on a warm November 27, Anderson hoped that the record book had been lost on the bus ride over.

In the opening quarter, the Dragons appeared to have done just that. On its second possession, Walker, behind the running of transfer tailback Gordon Pleasants and quarterback Alvin Harris, drove fifty-four yards on thirteen plays.

The 1976 game-day program. *Courtesy of Art Utley.*

Maggie Walker's Carroll Turner caps off the Green Dragon upset win in the 1976 Classic with a twelve-yard scoring return of a fumble recovery. *1977* Maggie L. Walker Dragon.

That thirteenth play was lucky, as Harris sneaked over from the one. Marvin Nappier kicked the PAT, and the Dragons took a 7–0 advantage as the period ended.

On the ensuing kickoff, William Brice lost control of the ball, and Michael Claudle recovered for the Dragons at the three. Wendell Jennings dropped Harris for a five-yard loss on first down, and Walker was forced to settle for Nappier's twenty-five-yard field goal, the only one ever kicked successfully in the history of the Classic, for a 10–0 lead with over eleven minutes left in the half.

That gave the Wildcats plenty of time to recover, and they did. On the next possession, Maurice Shands broke through a hole off left tackle and ran thirty-five yards to the Walker twenty-nine. Pushed back to the thirty-one, Shands went up the middle and crossed the goal line to pull Armstrong to 10–6.

Now it was Walker's time to turn the ball over as Pleasants fumbled a punt that Michael Floyd recovered.

With just three minutes and twenty seconds left before intermission, Shands broke free on an eighteen-yard touchdown run, and suddenly the Wildcats had roared back to take a 12–10 advantage.

In the third period, Walker's offense slowly began to reassert control of the game but failed to take advantage of several scoring opportunities.

Timeline Timeout

When he stepped onto the field on November 29, 1975, twenty Classics had been played since a young Lou Anderson ran out as senior receiver, appearing in his lone year of playing football at Maggie Walker. This time, he was in his fifth year as the Green Dragons' head coach. The problem for Anderson was that he had more wins over the Wildcats in one year as a player than in the four years he was the head coach.

The only head coach in the history of the Classic to have both played and coached in a game traveled a long road to get where he was.

After graduating from Walker in 1956, he headed to Kittrell College in North Carolina, where he played football and basketball for two years. Anderson then moved to Claflin College in South Carolina, where, while playing football and basketball, he graduated in 1961 with a degree in social studies. He ended up at L.P. Foster High School, the VIA school in Nottoway County, as an assistant coach.

As the VIA began to shut down in the late 1960s, Anderson returned to Walker and, in 1969, served as the Green Dragons' junior varsity coach. When the redistricting plan of 1970 was implemented, he found himself at Thomas Jefferson as the Vikings' junior varsity coach and head baseball coach.

Then Cooper retired from coaching at Walker, and Anderson was tapped as his replacement. The Dragons' program had been spread thin as players and students were distributed among seven schools. Starting from square one, Anderson and the Green Dragons went 4-5-0 in 1971, 2-7-0 in 1972 and 2-7-1 in 1973.

By1974, the record had improved to 6-2-1, but as with the three prior years, the season ended with the Dragons falling to the Wildcats in the Classic.

When the clock ran down on the 1975 game and Anderson looked up at the City Stadium scoreboard, he saw that it read "Maggie Walker: 33, Armstrong: 6" and would always know that he was a Classic champion, both on the field and on the sideline.

Inset picture: Lou Anderson, Maggie Walker head coach, 1971–78. *1977* Maggie L. Walker Dragon.

Some of the fifteen thousand spectators who gathered for the 1976 Classic. *1977* Maggie L. Walker Dragon.

After the Dragons had driven to the Wildcat eighteen and given the ball over on downs, disaster hit Armstrong.

When Armstrong quarterback Ralph Eagleton turned to pitch the ball to Tyrone Powell, he was hit by Claudle and middle guard Glenn Lewis. The ball sailed behind Powell and was picked up by Carroll Turner. Turner scampered twelve yards into the end zone, and suddenly the Dragons were up 16–12. Nappier connected on the PAT, and with four minutes and seven seconds left, Walker led 17–12.

As the clock finally reached zero, the Dragons had not only thrown the record book away, but they had also torn several pages out of it.

Questions over the eligibility of Pleasants, who was named the Classic's Most Valuable Player, arose. Having transferred from Hermitage High, Pleasants, a sophomore, had played in the Dragons' other win against Huguenot and in a tie with Lee-Davis. Both of those games were forfeited. Since the Armstrong game was played after the playoff cutoff, would it be included among the forfeits?

On February 25, 1977, it was announced that the Classic fell under the rules of the Virginia High School League, and the victory was awarded to Armstrong.

Maggie Walker	7	3	0	7	**17**
Armstrong	0	12	0	0	**12**

W: Harris one-yard run (Nappier kick)
W: Nappier twenty-five-yard field goal.
A: Shands thirty-one-yard run (run failed)
A: Shands eighteen-yard run (pass failed)
W: Turner twelve-yard fumble return (Nappier kick)

JUST GLAD TO GET OFF THE FIELD

November 26, 1977

Forty years. That's how much—or little—time had passed since a bunch of Maggie Walker underclassmen met a more experienced Armstrong eleven at Hovey field on a cold, cloudy Friday afternoon in 1938.

Between two and five thousand (depending on whom you talked to) saw the Wildcats' romp, 26–0. And not one person in the crowd bothered to report the game to any of the Richmond-area media outlets.

Since then, on nearly every Saturday after Thanksgiving, the two schools had lived and died and sometimes just settled for a tie over the game. Forty years later, just as in 1938, Armstrong was favored.

For the Wildcats, 1977 was a breakthrough season as Armstrong entered the Classic with eight wins, no losses and one tie, its best record since 1947, when it was crowned VIA state champions.

But there was no championship for this year's squad, as the ineligibility caused by the Classic's date gave the District Title to a 2-5-3 George Wythe team. In fact, Wythe was the lone team to blemish the Wildcats' record in a 6–6 tie.

For the Dragons, the memories of 1976 had been eased a little as Walker approached the Classic at 5-4-0. When game day arrived, a sparse (by Classic standards) crowd of ten thousand gathered at City Stadium on a raw, cold, wintry day.

There was little to keep them warm. After a scoreless opening period, it was the Wildcat defense that brought the fans to their feet in the second when, with

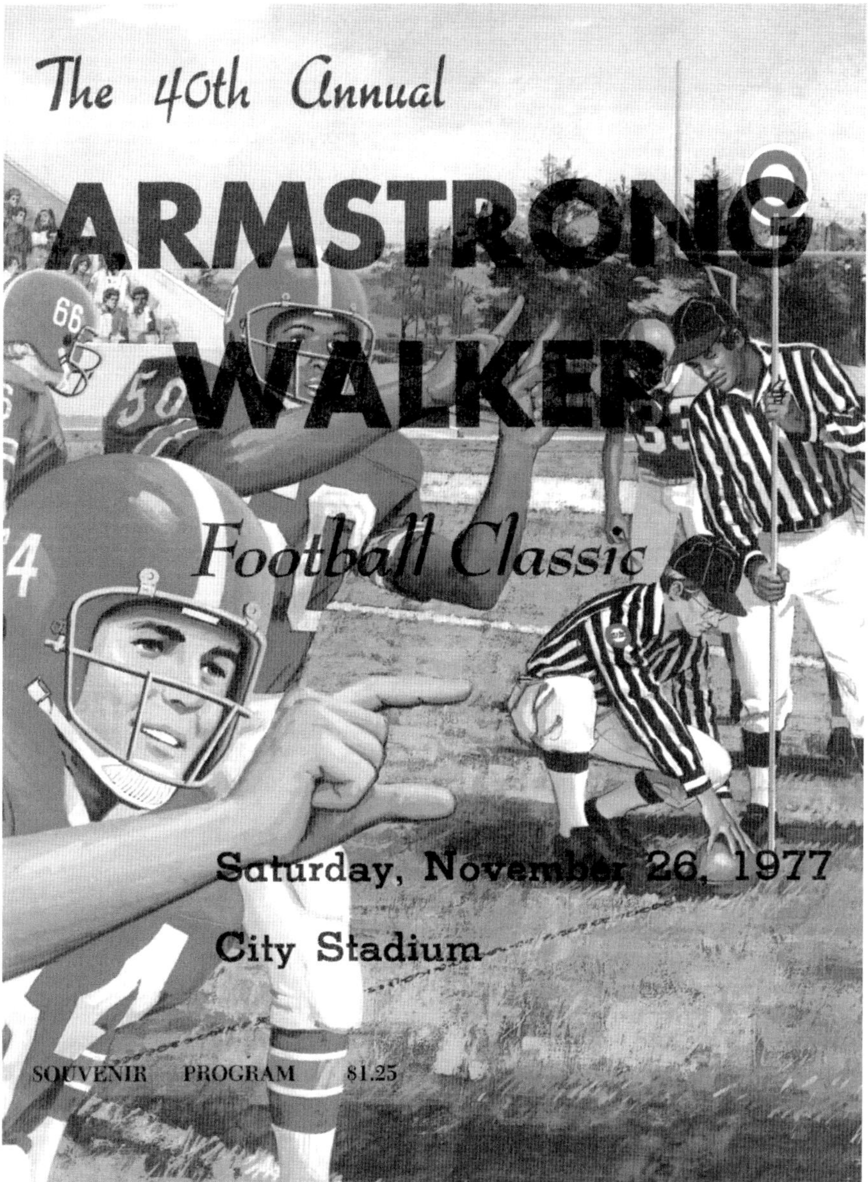

The 1977 game-day program. *Courtesy of Art Utley.*

The 1977 Armstrong football team. *1978* Armstrong Rabza.

about six minutes left before intermission, Walker tailback Gordon Pleasants, trying to get some yardage at his own thirteen, lost control of the ball.

As the ball bounced in and out of the hands of at least five players, Armstrong tackle Marion McMackle grabbed it at the six and ran in for the score. The Wildcats lined up for a two-point conversion attempt, and quarterback Ralph Eagleton broke the goal line. Armstrong went up 8–0.

The game returned to a defensive struggle, and the half ended with the Wildcats holding on to their one-touchdown advantage.

With the playing conditions showing no sign of improving in the third period, for a second time the Armstrong defense came up with a big play.

After the Wildcats had stopped the Dragon offense, Marvin Nappier was forced to set up in punt formation. As the ball reached Nappier, so did Armstrong end Vance Pittman, who got a hand on the ball. As it bounced at the Walker forty, Pittman picked up the pigskin and raced the rest of the way for the score. Although the conversion run failed, the Wildcats went up 14–0, and on this Saturday afternoon, that lead seemed to be enough to hold.

But this was the Classic. Early in the final period, sophomore quarterback Reynard Revels drove Walker to the Armstrong one before the Wildcats stiffened to take over on downs.

On the ensuing play, the Dragon defense broke through to nail Richard Pearson in the end zone for a safety, and the score stood at 14–2.

According to the rules, Armstrong free-kicked the ball from its twenty. Revels pulled in the ball and returned it to the Wildcat thirty-five.

Driving to the four, the Dragons scored when Al Hutchinson pulled a touchdown pass from Revels, and the two combined for the conversion as Walker pulled to 14–10.

It appeared that the Green Dragon comeback was going to be complete when Walker reached the Wildcat fourteen as time was running out.

But incomplete passes turned the ball over to the Wildcats, and two final Dragon possessions came up short. As time ran out, the Wildcat faithful ran out onto the field in celebration. But not for too long—it was just so cold.

Armstrong	0	8	6	0	**14**
Maggie Walker	0	0	0	10	**10**

A: McMackle six-yard fumble recovery (Eagleton run)
A: Pittman forty-yard blocked punt return (run failed)
W: Safety
W: Hutchinson four-yard pass from Revels (Hutchinson pass from Revels)

The Last Classic

November 25, 1978

For the forty-first year, Richmond woke up to a Classic matchup. The skies were clear, but the air was cool, and temperatures wouldn't get out of the forties. The *Richmond Times-Dispatch* reported on the front page that in the jungles of Guyana, more than 775 bodies of cultists had been recovered from the mass murder/suicide at Jonestown.

But it was page C-2 that hit home with Classic fans: it was finally over. At 2:00 p.m. that November 25, for the last time, there would be an opening kickoff for the annual Armstrong–Maggie Walker football game. After the 1978–79 school year, there would no longer be an Armstrong or Maggie Walker High School.

Faced with decreasing enrollment, the Richmond School Board had chosen to implement "Plan G" for the opening of the 1979 school year. Under this plan, athletic and other school programs at the seven city high schools would be consolidated into three. Armstrong and Church Hill rival J.F. Kennedy became the Armstrong-Kennedy Jaguars; Maggie Walker

The 1978 game-day program. *Courtesy of Eva Brinkley.*

and John Marshall merged to become the Marshall-Walker Cavaliers. The remaining three schools—Thomas Jefferson, Huguenot and George Wythe—were reorganized into the Jefferson-Huguenot-Wythe Trojans.

This plan had been announced earlier in the spring, so the fact that the 1978 Classic would be the last came as no surprise. Surprise or no, it didn't ease the sadness of losing a part of the fabric that held a community together and enriched an entire city.

Both squads had to put all the hype out of their minds, for they were the ones who would call the plays, carry the ball and make the hits.

For Maggie Walker, 1978 had been a return to strength after two off seasons as the Green Dragons entered the showdown 4-1-0 in the Capital District and 6-2-0 overall. Over at Armstrong, the memories of the undefeated 1977 season were just that—memories. The Wildcats stumbled to a 2-3-0 record in the district and stood at 3-6-0 overall.

As kickoff neared, the spectators began to file into the stands at City Stadium as they had since 1941. Walking on the field with over twenty-five thousand roaring fans in attendance, the more seasoned players and coaches smiled as they saw the look of awe on the faces of the first-time participants.

This was the Classic.

The underdog Wildcats opened the game massing on the line of scrimmage to nullify the running attack of the Green Dragons. Especially targeted was Gordon Pleasants, who had amassed 1,111 yards over eight games.

And for a while the plan worked, but just for a while.

Walker did break the ice in the opening quarter, but it was the Dragon defense that set things up. On their first possession, the Wildcats attempted a pitchout from quarterback Chris Daniels to Tyrone Powell. The connection was never made, and Alvin Harris, after trying several times to pick up the loose ball and run, decided to simply fall on it at the Armstrong seventeen.

Pleasants carried the ball four straight times to move it to the one, and quarterback Reynard Revels called his own number, scoring on a sweep to the left. The kick for the extra point failed, but the Dragons were up 6–0.

However, that was all there was in the first half of offense as the Wildcats, unable to move the ball, held the Dragons to just three first downs and thirty-eight yards of total offense.

By intermission, the crowd had grown to thirty thousand. This was indeed the Classic.

At halftime, the Walker coaching staff went to something old and something new. The old was a change of jerseys. When the Dragons took

Action in the 1978 Classic. *1979* Maggie L. Walker Dragon.

the field in the third period, the 1960s practice of wearing new jerseys in the second half was renewed. On the front was "Walker" and on the back, "41st Classic."

The new element was to get the ball to Pleasants.

The way to do that was to open up the Wildcat defense with a passing attack. On their first possession of the third quarter, the Dragons started at their own forty. Using a sequence of passes from Revels to Harris covering forty-two yards, Walker moved the ball to the Armstrong sixteen. From there, Pleasants got the call and, in one play, put the Dragons up 12–0.

As the period began to wind down, the Walker offense began to wind up for one last time.

Starting on their own twenty-three yard line, the Dragons reached the Wildcat thirty-one as the final quarter began. On the first play, Robert Smith took a reverse and raced into the end zone.

Leading 18–0, the Walker defense did the rest. Armstrong, having sputtered all season on offense, finished the contest with just fifty-five yards rushing, ten yards passing and just four first downs. The Wildcats' deepest penetration was the Dragon twenty-six in the second quarter.

Above: Maggie Walker defenders Matthew Liggans (number 1), Alvin Harris (number 7), Ernest Edmonds (number 64) and John Lewis (number 63) bring down an Armstrong running back in the 1978 Classic. *1979 Armstrong Rabza*.

Left: Maggie Walker's Thomas Mosley (number 66) and Ernest Edmonds (number 64) bring down an unidentified Armstrong running back in the 1978 Classic. *1979* Armstrong Rabza.

As the final seconds ticked off on the final period of the final Classic, a crowd estimated to number as many as forty-three thousand fans was in attendance.

That was the Classic.

Maggie Walker	6	0	6	6	**18**
Armstrong	0	0	0	0	**0**

W: Revels one-yard run (kick failed)
W: Pleasants sixteen-yard run (kick failed)
W: Smith thirty-one-yard run (kick failed)

The Postgame Wrap-Up

SEPTEMBER 7, 1979

Marshall-Walker defeated Armstrong-Kennedy 14–12 in the first post-Classic meeting.

APRIL 15, 1985

France Brinkley, longtime PA man for the Classic, passed away.

MAY 5, 1985

Arthur "Stretch" Gardner passed away.

1986

Willie Lanier (Maggie Walker, 1960–62) was inducted into the National Football League Hall of Fame.

FALL 1986

Plan G was reversed. Armstrong High reopened, but Maggie L. Walker High was renamed the Walker Building and housed the Richmond Open High School, the Richmond Community High School and the Arts and Humanities Center.

OCTOBER 5, 1989

Angier Lawrence passed away.

Leigh Street, 2009. *Photo by Michael Whitt.*

FALL 1990

Lou Anderson became the only person to have been head coach of both Maggie Walker and Armstrong, taking over at Armstrong for one season.

MAY 4, 1995

John "Pop" Williams passed away.

1998

Established in 1991, the Richmond Region Governor's School moved into the renovated Walker Building and was renamed the Maggie L. Walker Governor's School.

AUGUST 18, 2001

Fred "Cannonball" Cooper passed away.

2004

The Thirty-first Street Building for Armstrong was closed, and the student body merged a second time with John F. Kennedy. The building on Cool Lane was renamed New Armstrong, ending the history of the Classic.

APPENDIX

Maggie Walker-Armstrong

1938	Armstrong	26	Maggie Walker	0
1939	Armstrong	24	Maggie Walker	6
1940	Maggie Walker	14	Armstrong	6
1941	Armstrong	18	Maggie Walker	0
1942	Maggie Walker	7	Armstrong	6
1943	Maggie Walker	6	Armstrong	6
1944	Maggie Walker	20	Armstrong	0
1945	Maggie Walker	33	Armstrong	0
1946	Maggie Walker	6	Armstrong	6
1947	Armstrong	19	Maggie Walker	0
1948	Armstrong	7	Maggie Walker	6
1949	Armstrong	0	Maggie Walker	0
1950	Maggie Walker	6	Armstrong	0
1951	Maggie Walker	6	Armstrong	0
1952	Armstrong	27	Maggie Walker	7
1953	Armstrong	13	Maggie Walker	7
1954	Armstrong	0	Maggie Walker	0
1955	Maggie Walker	6	Armstrong	0

1956	Maggie Walker	6	Armstrong	0
1957	Maggie Walker	0	Armstrong	0
1958	Armstrong	14	Maggie Walker	7
1959	Maggie Walker	30	Armstrong	0
1960	Maggie Walker	12	Armstrong	7
1961	Armstrong	14	Maggie Walker	7
1962	Maggie Walker	27	Armstrong	13
1963	Maggie Walker	21	Armstrong	7
1964	Maggie Walker	19	Armstrong	13
1965	Maggie Walker	18	Armstrong	0
1966	Maggie Walker	14	Armstrong	7
1967	Maggie Walker	13	Armstrong	6
1968	Maggie Walker	18	Armstrong	6
1969	Maggie Walker	31	Armstrong	0
1970	Maggie Walker	18	Armstrong	12
1971	Armstrong	6	Maggie Walker	0
1972	Armstrong	34	Maggie Walker	0
1973	Armstrong	22	Maggie Walker	0
1974	Armstrong	24	Maggie Walker	22
1975	Maggie Walker	33	Armstrong	6
1976	Maggie Walker	17	Armstrong	12
1977	Armstrong	14	Maggie Walker	10
1978	Maggie Walker	18	Armstrong	0

Maggie Walker–Armstrong

Miss Armstrong		Miss Walker	
1938	Ethel Louise Howell	1938	Unavailable
1939	Sarah Bebbs Frend	1939	Mattie Roane
1940	Martha Stewart	1940	Unavailable
1941	Gwen Coles	1941	Eva Webber Rueben
1942	Allie Lewis Richardson	1942	Lelia Dickerson Kersey
1943	Vivian Boisseau	1943	Lucille Jacobs
1944	Aurelia Eggleston Ford	1944	Delcenia McCullum
1945	Jean Freeman Barnes	1945	Margaret Smith
1946	Page Turner	1946	Dorothy Hopkins
1947	Grace Ford	1947	Lucy Chatman
1948	Doris Dandridge	1948	Edna Theresa Carpenter Woolridge
1949	Merry Patterson Stovall	1949	Viola Milford
1950	Evora Williams Jones	1950	Ellen Miles
1951	Elizabeth Lambert Jones	1951	Delia Anderson
1952	Delores Williamson Whitaker	1952	Josephine Laughorne
1953	Frances Frey LeGrade	1953	Jane Bates
1954	Ivy Hopkins McLaughlin	1954	Evelyn Hinton
1955	Janice Scales Jeter	1955	Gusrava Brown
1956	Sadie Thomas Norrell	1956	Anne Burgess
1957	Ann Price	1957	Ernestine Walker
1958	Sylvia Jeter Lambert	1958	Jacqueline Coleman
1959	Ester White	1959	Lorretta Smith
1960	Alease Sully	1960	Angella Current
1961	Audrey Freeman	1961	Yvonne Anderson
1962	Grace Tolliver	1962	Gwendolyn Leecost
1963	Audrey Stevens	1963	Carolyn Branch
1964	Sharletta Branch	1964	Janet Foster
1965	Charlene Mills	1965	Beverly Paige Pervall Johnson

1966 Linda Smith
1967 Gwendolyn Daniels
1968 Suzette Tomlin
1969 Shelis Bishop
1970 Brenda Caudle
1971 Vera Harvey
1972 Brenda Hawkins
1973 Cecelia Graham
1974 Ivy Hutchinson
1975 Cheryl Rowe
1976 Debra Crosby
1977 Adriene Davis
1978 Francis Jean Carter

1966 Lisbeth Sharon Thompson
1967 Roselyn Brooks
1968 Jacqueline Victoria Henley
1969 Mildred Janet Watson
1970 Wanda Shelton
1971 Beverly Satchell
1972 Mildred Hilton
1973 Denise Britt
1974 Chris Watson
1975 Renee Jones
1976 Lisa Sloan
1977 Donna Shipskinski
1978 Denise Wilson